Getting Them Sober, Volume Three

Also by Toby Rice Drews:

Getting Them Sober, Volume One
    (also available on audiocassette)
Getting Them Sober Action Guide
Getting Them Sober, Volume Two
Getting Them Sober, Volume Three
Get Rid of Anxiety and Stress
The 350 Secondary Diseases/Disorders to Alcoholism

Getting Them Sober, Volume 3

Toby Rice Drews

Bridge Publishing, Inc.
Publishers of
LOGOS • HAVEN • OPEN SCROLL

Getting Them Sober, Volume Three
Copyright © 1986 by Toby Rice Drews
All rights reserved
Printed in the United States of America
Library of Congress Catalog Card Number: 85-073330
International Standard Book Number 0-88270-603-9
Bridge Publishing, Inc.
2500 Hamilton Blvd.
South Plainfield, NJ 07080

Contents

Section One

1 Family "Gang-Up" Against
   the Non-Alcoholic Parent 1

2 Is Alcoholism a Moral Issue? 18

3 If You Are an Adult Child of an
   Alcoholic, *and* are Married to an
   Alcoholic, Don't Compare Your
   Progress in Treatment With Those
   Who Had a "Normal Upbringing" 26

4 When Recovered Alcoholics Who
   Need to Go to Al-Anon
   Hesitate to Do So 34

5 We Attach So Much Importance
   to What He Says and Does 43

6 For the Man Involved With
   a Woman Alcoholic 52

7 If You're Bored by Nice Men,
   or If You're "Just Going With"
   an Alcoholic 62

8   If You're a Helping Professional
Who Has Clients Who Are Both
Alcoholics *and* Spouses of Alcoholics....... 72

9   Dealing With Your Alcoholic Child
When Your Spouse Also
Has a Drinking Problem..................... 81

10   From "Pity to Punish".......................... 89

11   Why Do I Have to Go to Al-Anon?
I *Know* What to Do Now! 101

12   More on Detachment.......................... 107

13   The Alcoholic Is So Very Predictable........ 116

Section Two

      Acknowledgments..................... 127

      Introduction........................... 129

      Foreword 135

      Preface 137

14   Interview with Dick Prodey, C.A.C. 141

15   Chronic Neuropsychiatric Disorders 152

16   Medical/Surgical Disorders 155

17   Sleep Disorders............................ 156

18   Peripheral and Autonomic Disorders........ 159

19   Myopathy 161

20   Musculoskeletal Disturbances 163

21   Liver and Pancreas Disorders............... 164

22 Gastrointestinal Disorders 168

23 Malnutrition and Related
     Nutritional Deficiencies 170

24 Infectious Diseases 173

25 Skin Diseases 177

26 Effects of Alcohol on
     the Hematopoietic System 180

27 Reproductive System Disorders 182

28 Effects on the Fetus 184

29 Endocrine Disturbances 185

30 Respiratory System Disorders 186

31 Cardiovascular System Disorders 188

32 Trauma and Surgery Problems 190

33 Psychiatric Disorders and Alcoholism 192

SECTION ONE

1

Family "Gang-Up" Against the Non-Alcoholic Parent

What if your alcoholic teen-ager decides to live with the alcoholic spouse you are separated from?

What if the drinking alcoholic you're separated from turns your grown children against you?

What do you do when the alcoholic goes to live with another family rescuer?

When there is the threat of another rescuer, all persons in an alcoholic family are afraid: of being shown up as failures; that even if they're not failures, "others" will think they are; that the alcoholic we care about will be in pain and/or die.

Let's take a look at one family's situation. Caroline's seventeen-year-old son, Steve, had four strong, witty, talented, attention-getting older sisters; he was quiet. He smoked pot and drank. He didn't get into much trouble; he just came home looking "pie-eyed." Caroline began to despair. Steve was the last of her five kids, and all of them had had problems.

His father was drinking himself to death, and telling his mother that he "didn't have a problem because he still had his job." He lost it later, but by then he *couldn't* stop drinking.

Steve was a likable person—he'd do anything for anyone. But he felt torn between his parents: no one spoke badly of his father; everyone knew he "had a disease," but nonetheless Steve felt everyone's anger towards his father. At the same time, he felt sorry for him. He seemed to know how badly his father was really hurting—that he was drinking because he *wouldn't* stop; it was because he *couldn't* stop.

Steve understood the rest of his family too. He understood that they had been so terribly hurt by his father for so many years that they couldn't feel anything but anger, and the pain his father's disease had inflicted upon them. He knew it wasn't just the drinking that had hurt them so much, the loss of money, of husband, of father—it was the cruel "games" his drunk mouth had played on them, all those years, so repetitiously.

His father would never remember these games even if he got sober, but his family remembered. Anyone would have trouble forgetting, much less forgiving. Steve *knew* all this instinctively; he didn't "know" he knew it, he just *knew* it. But he was the youngest and the most hooked into terrible feelings of pity for his dad. He ached for him.

When Caroline separated from Bill, Steve told her, "Mom, I want to go live with dad."

2

Caroline was so worried that Bill would now have a drinking buddy, that her son's drinking would get worse because of all the every-day drinking that would go on. She was afraid her family would not understand her "allowing" her son to go. (Let *them* try to control a headstrong, drinking, teen-aged son.)

Also, she was afraid of feeling like a failure, that *she* couldn't control her son. Even though she was in a support group for families of alcoholics, she couldn't let go of these feelings, especially around her children. It was much easier to "let go" of her husband to see him as an adult who was responsible for himself. But not her babies. No, they weren't "babies." They were teen-agers. But, they were *her* babies. She had always wanted them. She loved having them, raising them. She loved every minute of it. Almost.

Those kids had kept her going. When her husband's disease plunged her into the deepest depression, it was the kids needing breakfast, needing their hair combed, their socks on, their shoes tied, that helped her through the day.

And now Steve, her youngest child, wanted to live with his father. Although this didn't happen all the time, her husband did a bit of gloating over the fact that her son preferred him—the "bad one"—to *her*—the "good one," as he called her. But mostly he just wanted the company. Her husband had retreated into solitary drinking and loneliness since his driver's license had been suspended for "driving under the influence." His favorite bar was near his workplace, and besides, it was cheaper by the case. And he had finally gotten to the point his other friends had reached: the point where, as he had said so often, "I'll sure stop if I get that bad." He was there, and he couldn't stop. Not now.

As it turned out, Steve was lucky. Frightened by witnessing close-up what would happen if he continued drinking, he decided to get help. He went to counseling and alcohol education. To this day, Steve hasn't had another drink.

Another family experienced similar difficulties. The wife's name is Samantha. What if your situation is like hers? What if, as Samantha told me, "My husband 'buys' our kids. He's got the business we worked all those years to put together. It's in his name. And the kids all work for him. I certainly don't want to take 'my share,' and break up the business. It's doing well. I get money from it too. It's just that since our separation, he's convinced the kids that *I'm* the crazy one, that I'm the one who's always 'seeing things'—yeah, like his drunks and his mistresses. The kids drink with him, except for Carol, our oldest, who doesn't drink, and doesn't really approve of his drinking. But she's bought off, too, because he buys her whatever she wants. And my husband gives her new furniture, a new car every other year. So, you see, *I'm* the nag."

What I find works well is a completely hands-off strategy: You stop talking about the alcoholic's behavior *entirely*. It's terribly difficult to do this, but what can keep you at it is knowing that the long-term goal is easily reached. In other words, if you act as if you no longer care what he's doing, how he's doing it, with whom he's doing it (with the kids or other women or your Aunt Sara), and just "wear blinders" and go about your business, discussing how you feel with *no one* but Al-Anon people and/or your counselor (because others will unwittingly give you the wrong advice or make you feel scared or guilty) within weeks, or, at the most, months, very probably your children, at least one of them, will begin to get turned around.

The sign will be that your child will start to complain to you of his father's behavior. (The same complaints that you made previously, and were called "crazy" when you said them.) *It is very important that, at this point, you do not go for the bait and agree, by saying, "Now, do you see what I've been through?"*

Say nothing. Shrug it off. *Don't gloat.* (Not on the surface, anyway.) You still have your feelings, of course, and being new at this behavior, you will understandably feel that this is a power play. You might even feel that you are beginning to "win." (I wouldn't pay too much attention to your feelings, though, because they can get you into trouble. Those gloating feelings can turn so easily into guilt *about* those feelings, and just result in a lot of confusion for you. Simply acknowedge that you have them; as best you can, ignore them.)

At this point, your child will probably escalate his "telling tales" about his father's behavior. Also, another of your children may start to "come over." It is at this point that I would calmly say that you can see that their father's behavior may be disturbing to them, and it used to be disturbing to you, but you've learned that you can't change your husband, you can change only your reaction to him. It would also be advisable to point out that you've learned this in Al-Anon, and/or counseling. It is here that you will want to suggest that they try a meeting or two. *No pressure, just an invitation.*

Now your child will probably have one or two reactions to your response: (1) Anger that you've "let daddy get away with this by not complaining," feeling that your detachment is "letting your husband get away with it." (2) Concern about his father's drinking, concern that he'll die. If the latter is your child's reaction, give him a good book on the disease concept of alcoholism to show him how very serious it is and about the hereditary factor. (One such book is *Under the Influence* by Dr. James Milam, a Bantam paperback.) This book will also tell your child something about his own drinking, if he drinks. *Follow up by reinviting him to Al-Anon so he can learn how to help his father.*

If your child is angry about his father "getting away with it," try to explain how your detachment from your husband's problem is *not* "letting him get away with it." That, instead, it's the best way in which you can *all* get well. This concept is known as "the beneficent circle of detachment." At first, you had to pretend you didn't care how he hurt you. Your "making believe" led, in turn, to a *true* detaching from what he did. You really began to pay attention to what made *you* feel good in your day instead of always watching what he was doing, and basing your opinion of yourself on what he said about you. *That* helped you to start really feeling good about yourself. Like all alcoholics, your husband used his "radar," and he "picked up on" your detachment, consequently becoming rather scared of it.

Why? Because previously, to feel good temporarily, he could puff himself up at your expense, but you have stopped that game. He then begins to try it on others—or else he has to focus on himself (and he's too scared to do that, because then he'll have to think about his drinking). As a result, he "dumps on" the kids for the first time, and starts to show *them* "his true colors." They, in response, confront him and his drinking for the first time.

Then you show your kids how to detach. When this happens he'll have *no one* to escape to or to "dump on," and there will be no one but him and his disease. It is at this point that he'll have to face it. That's how detachment helps everybody.

Even if all the kids don't detach themselves, he'll probably listen more to *their* telling him about his drinking, as opposed to *you* telling him, because he's not as alienated yet from them, and is still trying to woo them. Who knows? Maybe one of them *will* be effective in telling him. The point is that everyone has a chance to win if the beneficent circle of detachment has a chance to begin.

What if your alcoholic teen-ager goes to live with another family rescuer? Oh, what *failure* that implies! Oh, what *guilt* that engenders!

Are they *right? Was* I a failure? Of course not! But were they right, a little bit? Am I possibly wrong when I said Timmy is an *alcoholic?* Even the *doctor* said he is—but are we *wrong? Will he show his alcoholism to his grandma?*

Absolutely.

Frances's husband, Ted, was a "silly" alcoholic. He wasn't arrogant; he wasn't nasty. He just didn't work at a job, just went out every day and said he wouldn't drink, and came home drunk. She'd *had* it!

Having not come from an alcoholic environment before her marriage, Frances was a pretty intact person. She never believed she should "put up with it." Her parents were wonderful; her father had hardly missed a day's work in forty years. Frances didn't think she had caused her husband's alcohol problem. She *knew* who had the problem.

She had none of the traditional double dose of guilt that adult children of alcoholics have when they marry alcoholics. Therefore, when her neighbor Dee told her, "If he was *my* husband, *I'd* be able to straighten him out!" Frances had the perfect answer: "Take him!"

This way she'd be able to get some rest! She would take the children to the shore for the weekend! But, first, she made Dee promise to keep her husband for a whole week. Dee righteously agreed.

While Frances and the children were at the beach, Dee counseled Ted earnestly all night. He listened intently, nodding and smiling wisely. After she went to bed, so smug that she had accomplished what Frances had not been able to do in years, Ted crept to the basement bar and devoured the contents by 7:00 A.M.

Frances heard Dee at the door of their beachfront apartment at 11:00 A.M.: "Frances! Open up! It's me, Dee! *Take* him! He's terrible!"

"No, dear. You wanted him. You promised to keep him for a week. You've got him," Frances answered.

She and the children had a peaceful week.

I have never heard of a situation where, if an alcoholic relative went to live with another family member, the person did not eventually come to understand that the person they took in, or tried to rescue, had a problem that was bigger than all of them.

This, of course, takes *time*. It won't happen overnight. In the immediate beginning of the "rescue operation," the relative will do a lot of fussy gloating. This will be followed by a period of telling you, by letter or phone, "everything is going very, very well," followed by a period of panic, frantic vacillating between crises—vacillating between blaming the alcoholic, and blaming you for not having done enough in years past and, therefore, "setting the scene" for all this present misery.

Next will come a period during which the relative will demand your help in the rescue operation (either with money, legal entanglements or your time). This will be followed by the relative asking you how you stood it all these years. All these stages will be repeated *over and over again,* until they are finally followed by the relative attempting to wash his hands, too. Often this is followed by a period of renewed rescue attempts by the relative or another rescuer who follows in the previous rescuer's stead.

All of this (if you don't attend Al-Anon to help you get through it) will engender *tremendous* amounts of guilt in you and *tremendous* self-doubt as to whether *you did enough.* And, if you don't learn how to detach yourself from all this, it can make you physically ill and emotionally exhausted.

What happened to John and his wife, Edna (who is the adult child of two alcoholics, and full of unfinished guilt about her parents, much less the guilt about their son's alcoholism), when their son, Jamie, decided to go live with grandma, "who understood"?

In the time before he went to live with his grandmother, Jamie had gone to college for six months. He got terrible grades because he drank all the time. He also lied a lot, and eventually dropped out after being on school probation. He made a point of saying he didn't "flunk"—it was just that no one "had given him a chance." His father got him a job in which he also failed, saying it "just wasn't his thing."

After all this, in just one and a half years, John and Edna decided to no longer foot the bill for Jamie's college education—at least not until Jamie got help for his drinking, attended AA regularly and was sober at least one year.

When he learned this, Jamie had a fit. He said he was moving to grandma's. (He had already spoken to her, and she had agreed to buy him a car and promised him that he'd never have to work while he was studying.)

Jamie moved in with grandma. Within one year he became bored. He secretly married someone he had met while drinking, someone who was "exciting." He then managed to convince his grandparents that he was doing well in school, and that he just needed "to stay out a lot to study." Before long, he dropped out of school again.

He conned his grandparents out of more tuition money the next semester (and more money to live "by himself"). He dropped out of school again. This time he called his parents to complain that his grandparents were too strict, moved back home with his new wife, convinced his grandparents that he had married because he was so lonely for his friends back home, had another car accident which he blamed on being too tired, and received a promise from his grandmother that she would give him enough money to live on for one year while he and his wife got themselves together and decided what to do with their lives.

Since that time nothing has changed. The last I heard, the situation had actually worsened.

Dealing with this is not easy. Without help, it is almost impossible. You can intellectually *know* the right things to do, but the guilt sets in so fiercely that head knowledge, alone, doesn't amount to a hill of beans.

What you *can definitely* expect from regular attendance at Al-Anon is a lessening of your guilt feelings, replaced by a certainty that you are *not* abandoning your child to the wolves when you stop worrying. Instead, you've learned to "let go and let God," which is a *lot* more potent an answer than you can expect to have alone.

You can (as my mother used to say) beat your head against a brick wall for another year—but *have* you been able to control your alcoholic teen-ager, yet? If you could have, you would have done it by now.

If it's not working, why not try the way that does work?

By the way, it's usually not enough just to pray. Because if you aren't in a group with others who understand what living with an alcoholic is like, you will start to feel guilty and start to feel that you could have prevented it. All of this does nothing but make you feel even more depressed, guilty, and immobilized, and therefore ineffective. We are not on this earth to live in those negative feelings, mostly because they keep us self-centered, and truly unable to help others *effectively!*

If you attend Al-Anon, your child will have an 80 percent better chance to get sober and *stay* sober than ever before.

Write On:

1. Do you believe that others can make your teenager into an alcoholic? (Can they make him into a diabetic? They're both real *diseases).*

2. Do you realize that alcoholism has its *own* dynamic? That if your son drinks, his disease will progress, whether or not he lives with his father or whether or not the world does as he wishes it would?

3. Write up creative ways in which you can, *in a very practical sense,* turn your attention off what the alcoholic is doing and/or saying.

Suggested Activity:
  Tell yourself, every day, that *guilt* is *your* disease.

2
Is Alcoholism a Moral Issue?

Just because alcoholism is a disease does not mean that you have to excuse the *behavior* and say, "Well, he's got a disease, so I'll overlook it." As a matter of fact, the less you overlook it, and the less you excuse it, the more you treat *yourself* as the most important person in that relationship—the better the chance the alcoholic has for recovery.

No, what we're talking about here is not excuses—what we're focusing on is the fact that alcoholism is not *caused* by moral problems. And that is not a theoretical issue. To believe that alcoholism is primarily a moral issue is killing alcoholics and their families. *If you treat the mental problems first, and not say "stop drinking" first, an alcoholic can do well in therapy for ten years and still die from alcoholism.*

Kathy called me from Denver and wanted to know what to do with her abusive husband who wouldn't leave home. And, she felt *she* couldn't leave. There were a lot of other problems coming from the alcoholism, too—gross physical problems for which she had been in treatment for more than ten years. Kathy also had a debilitating depression that came from not being able to leave the situation.

I asked her, "Are you going to Al-Anon?"

"I went once, but I didn't go back. I can't," she answered.

"Why in the world not?" I asked.

"They're not Christians there!" she cried.

"Kathy, if you had a heart attack, and were taken to the hospital by paramedics, would you yell when you got there, 'Wait! Is the doctor a Christian?' "

"No," she answered in a small, confused voice. "But, they talk about God, and they don't say, 'Jesus.' "

"Kathy, do you think Jesus would dislike anything that is said in Al-Anon to comfort the families of alcoholics, and give them tools that work in an effort to help themselves and the alcoholic?"

"No," she said. "I guess not. But, there are all kinds of people there. And they talk about the 'God of your understanding,' and I know that *that's* Jesus."

"Kathy, let me tell you how I see this, and possibly I can help you work it out. First, AA and Al-Anon don't see themselves as the final word on spirituality. Bill Wilson, one of the two co-founders of AA talked about AA being just a 'spiritual kindergarden.'

"AA urges people to make peace with churches in which they were reared. It doesn't ever presume to be *the* spiritual or religious answer; it *says* it would

19

be wrong and arrogant to do so. It is often said that 'God brings you to AA, and AA brings you back to God.' Kathy, you certainly can't be redeemed by Christ if you're dead from alcoholism.

"And I know that there are some who would say that it is better for a man to die from alcoholism than to be saved from dying and not become a Christian. But, for myself, I don't think I have the right to make a decision like that for another human being. Besides, who's to say what a man will do once he's conscious? Can I predict whether he'll find his way, eventually, or not? At least, if he doesn't die, he'll have a chance. I don't have the right to condemn anyone to die an alcoholic death. I know that we family members get so angry that we don't care whether they die, at times; but that keeps *us* sick. For a very selfish reason I try to let go of my resentments, because I don't want to become ill from them.

"My resentments feel good at the time (they make me feel puffed up and morally superior, but I usually fall soon thereafter). *Something* happens to bring me up short and show me I'm not what I thought I was, when I was feeling good at someone else's expense. And, I find that I'm in a chronic, low-level depression when I'm fueled by nagging resentment. I'm just tired of it. That doesn't mean I have to choose to live with another person's crazies! As a matter of fact, it means the opposite! If I keep putting myself in a position to be negatively affected by another person, then *that* will fuel the resentment. No, if I find that the sick person wants to stay that way—for whatever reason—I have the God-given right to remove myself from that situation, whatever way that is."

Kathy went to Al-Anon and did just what they say to do: "Take what you like, and leave the rest." She took the practical advice on how to deal with alcoholism as a disease, and continued to go to church to fill her spiritual needs. It's the same thing she would do if she had diabetes—she'd go to a diabetes doctor to treat the disease, without expecting him to meet her spiritual needs. Kathy's husband is now sober.

What do we mean, then, when we say that alcoholism is a disease?

We mean that many people can pick up a drink for social or religious reasons, and put it down, and forget about it. Alcoholics drink for many of the same reasons most people drink, at first. But alcoholics have alterations in brain chemistry and in the enzyme system that are activated when they drink even moderately. At some time in his or her drinking, the allergy/craving will start; i.e., the alcoholic will, at one and the same time, physiologically crave, *need,* alcohol—and become violently ill from it, too.

Now, if you were as drugged as an alcoholic is (alcohol is a drug, and all alcoholics are drug addicts) your behavior, too, would become warped. *Anyone's* would.

21

When the alcoholic recovers in AA, he or she must use the Twelve Steps of that program to recover his relationship with his "Higher Power" in order to heal those areas where he was driven and self-occupied by alcohol-induced unknown terrors. He must become "weller than well" as they say in AA, so that when the very tough times come, he will not look for immediate chemical relief as his neighbor can do (the one who can take a tranquilizer when his child dies; the one who can have a drink on a long plane trip; the one who can take a sleeping pill when an earthquake shatters the home he built). For the alcoholic, that first drink or pill would set in motion the alcoholism once again. We live in a world that demands, and gets, immediate gratification. So, the alcoholic, when recovered in AA, isn't necessarily more "sick" than others; he just *has* to be in touch with a power outside himself for the relief that a drink or a pill used to give him. He has to switch from a chemical death-style to a spiritual power.

Write On:

1. Have you ever switched churches, homes or neighborhoods out of shame, because of alcoholism?

2. Are you aware that *every* time you or I act as if alcoholism is a disease and not a shame, it helps foster the realization that it *is* a disease, and therefore makes it easier for all of us to reach out for help and not die? Write about instances you may remember in your family history where alcoholism was considered to be a condemnation rather than a sickness.

Suggested Activity:

Tell yourself, each time you feel ashamed of what alcoholics in your family are doing, that: (1) They have a disease; (2) it is not *your* disease; and (3) his treatment for that disease often begins when you hand his disease back to him.

3

If You Are an Adult Child of an Alcoholic, *and* Are Married to an Alcoholic, Don't Compare Your Progress in Treatment With Those Who Had a "Normal Upbringing"

A woman who had owned her own farm equipment business for over five years called me recently. She became ill for six months, and could not run her business on a full-time basis. She and her husband had been saving their money to send him back to graduate school. Because of her illness, and because she was able to run the business only part-time, his schooling had to be put off for two years, since they had to dip into their savings to keep things going. (He worked, too, but they needed her income.)

When she obviously wasn't ready to return to work full-time after the first two months of the illness, her husband told her, "You obviously don't care about my education we've been saving for. If you're not willing to work, *now,* full-time, I'm leaving you." She still had four months of convalescence, according to her doctor.

Her husband had convinced her that he was right, until she went into Al-Anon, and also had a time of physical separation from him. What made her feel particularly crazy, she told me, was that underneath, she knew it was right to be angry at him, and yet at the same time, she hated herself for believing him.

This woman is an adult child of an alcoholic *and* is married to a drinking alcoholic.

She, like most adult children of alcoholics, never learned to be emotionally intact or appropriate in her behavior or thinking. Alcoholic-family expectations are all-or-nothing deals, where we think, one minute, that we will never feel hurt or pain again because we feel so "wonderful." And the next minute, we think we are falling apart—that the pain is so bad, it will never pass, and that we "can't stand it."

When you marry an alcoholic, on top of coming from an alcoholic family, it's as if you had an old, painful fracture that never quite healed and someone kept battering it, sometimes hard, sometimes soft, for twenty years. The pain would never end totally; sometimes it would subside, and you'd think things are better. You would become used to it, and it would seem normal. You would forget—or never know— what fracture-free life was like.

I believe that a rough road is tread by adult children of alcoholics who marry alcoholics. We feel joy, pain, grief, fear, and wonder more intensely than others usually do. That's a double-edged sword. One can learn to mitigate it, live with it, accept it, and let Al-Anon heal much of it. Some of it stays, and we can learn to love the part that stays.

A recovering alcoholic nun, who counsels many recovering sisters, told me how she has learned to accept being a "wounded healer." One of the promises of AA is that we will "not regret the past nor wish to shut the door on it." Perhaps this is true for adult children of alcoholics, also.

We learn to build a protective bubble around us because we have no choice but to develop that bubble, for we are such sensitive people. We can "see" even when they *intend* to injure us. How do we get that bubble? As we go through the pain, we take no mind-altering drugs to mask the pain in order to get us through to the other side. We pray for the person who injures us. We call someone and tell that person how much anger we feel. We exercise our bodies. We throw something in a vacant lot. We go to a counselor or a healing group that teaches us we are not trapped—that even if we cannot do so *now,* we *will* be able to free ourselves in the future. At first, it is in the form of hope; then we *know* it is true when we begin to see progress in the form of small things we could not do before. We begin to see our options.

On the other side, we see that our super-sensitivity is a bonus! If we are in the helping professions, we can almost "read" our clients and "get inside their skins." Often we can help them in ways it may take other clinicians *years* to learn. We can learn to ride the crest of the waves that threaten to overwhelm us when we experience our *intense* joys. We no longer have to fear intensity. When we begin to *accept* and enjoy the present moments of the crests, we are let down ever so much more gently, peacefully.

When we are in groups of similar persons who understand—Al-Anon, Al-Ateen, AA—we no longer fear emotional pain so much. We *know* that "this, too, shall pass." We learn that our fears of the pain made the pain double in intensity.

We are also beginning to know detachment.

We become more patient *with ourselves*. (This is not to be confused with putting up with unacceptable behavior of others.) We start to *know* that it took a long time for our behavior and thinking patterns to develop—and it will take time to change them. *But we begin to see the healing!*

At first, it was a leap of faith—a realization that we could not go on any more in the old way. It hurt too much. *That* got us to recovery groups. We just hoped "it" would all get better as they told us. But then we started *seeing* it! We began to feel better in ways we never expected!

But some of us forgot to be patient with ourselves.

We began to compare our progress, not with *ourselves,* but with the progress of others.

We forgot that we were comparing our progress, as persons who *always* lived with alcoholism, with people who were blessed with intactness for the formative eighteen to twenty years of their lives.

When someone calls me and asks, "What am I doing wrong? I've been in the program for three months, and I'm not making as much headway towards peace as two others who are newer than I am in the group," or another one may ask, "What more should I do? Should I go to intensive therapy, too?" I realize that, invariably, I am dealing with adult children of alcoholics. *Some* progress is never enough. We want it all *yesterday*—and, if we got it all yesterday, we would feel an emptiness, and a fear.

Healing *needs* to be slower than our racing minds. We need to keep it very simple, especially when we are in our first year of support groups. Do you have a sponsor? (Someone you can call five times a day, if you need to?) Do you have phone numbers of people in your group? If not, are you willing to ask for them? *Remember, your calling them helps them get better!* (They're not doing you a favor! Helping *you* helps *them* to get well!)

Unless your situation is unusual, or life-threatening, it is often a good idea to stick to the program of Al-Anon and/or AA for six months to a year before attempting professional counseling because we are mostly so shaky when we come into the program and so vulnerable that we are easily confused. And, if you are not fortunate enough to get a counselor who understands the total disease of alcoholism, progress can be hindered. There's no way that you will be steered wrongly in AA/Al-Anon, because these programs present principles over personalities. If one or more persons turns you off, and doesn't seem helpful, "take what you like and leave the rest," as Al-Anon says, and find the people who can help you. Pray about it; the right people will be put into your path.

Write On:

If you are an adult child of an alcoholic, and if you also married an alcoholic, and if you have described your situation to someone who has never lived with alcoholism, write about how they reacted, and told you how bizarre it must be for you to live in that situation.

Suggested Activity:

Each time you remember that the situation is bizarre, tell yourself:

(1) You are *not* imagining how bizarre/crazy it is.

(2) Families make molehills out of mountains—our illness makes *us* feel we are exaggerating.

(3) You are not strange for getting caught up in it—it is *normal* for *normal* people to feel like the *abnormal* ones when living with an alcoholic.

4

When Recovered Alcoholics Who Need to Go to Al-Alon Hesitate to Do So

Two-thirds or more of the persons in the rooms of Alcoholics Anonymous meetings are deeply concerned about another family member's drinking.

Why, then, does one see only a tiny sprinkling of those persons who are in need, in the Al-Anon rooms? Alcoholics who are worried about other family members certainly are needy and hurting terribly. And, in many cases, when they are newly sober also, their sobriety is sometimes unnecessarily jeopardized because they are not getting the tools they need to detach themselves comfortably from the threats (covert and overt) that come from living with another person's drinking.

Four objections one hears about recovered alcoholics who contemplate attending Al-Anon are:

1. "What do you need *that* for? You've *got* your program!" (in AA).

2. "All they talk about is how bad alcoholics are!"

(Is that an alcoholic's contempt before investigating Al-Anon? Or, is it true?)

3. "Al-Anon? Oh, that's just the girls in the back room."

4. "Don't confuse yourself. Keep it simple. You just need to stay sober. Don't go to more than one twelve-step program. You'll just muddy up the waters. *Don't worry about that guy you're living with! Just stay sober and it'll work out!*"

Let's look at these objections.

Bill Wilson, one of the co-founders of AA, was adamant, over and over again, in saying that AA did not have the only answer to everything in the world. He saw a psychiatrist for many years after being in AA and said that psychiatric treatment had helped him tremendously. I'm certain he would not object to anything which benefits one's spiritual program and helps one become more serene and get a calmer life. He wrote, often warning people, about the dangers of arrogance and shortsightedness and thinking that we alcoholics are the be-all and end-all of life.

Recovered alcoholics don't get competitive feelings about church-going. They don't feel defensive about recovered alcoholics attending group therapy for families of cancer victims if their child has cancer. Why, then, does their hair frequently rise when Al-Anon is mentioned?

Some of those who feel threatened by alcoholics attending Al-Anon may be thinking along the following lines:

"I divorced that miserable woman long ago. She'd make a great Al-Anon! Complaining about my behavior the whole time I was drinking!" (Is there an amends-making that's been put off too long? Or even if amends *were* made, is there unfinished business, in the sense of terrible uncomfortableness, going on?)

Look, we can all understand if this is so. Who in the world *doesn't* have skeletons in the closet? Who hasn't treated someone in the past in a shabby way and still hasn't forgiven oneself, or perhaps claimed the bad treatment was justified? *However, is this a good reason, if we are honest with ourselves, to tell someone else not to go to a program that may just help them to stay calm enough to get through a terrible struggle with early sobriety?*

Lydia is a woman who has been sober in AA for ten years now. Her husband also has been sober in AA for ten years. They live in Texas. On the phone she told me how, when she was in early sobriety, she could not be around her husband for a very long time without terrible hostility rising in her, resulting in her wanting to drink. She usually just avoided him, and went to work and to a lot of AA meetings. This would work fine until she and her husband would be on vacation together. Then the "stuff" would start. He would be on vacation and at home. She would be on vacation and also would spend it at home. They'd be like two porcupines around each other.

What she did to solve this problem was to attend Al-Anon every day while she was on vacation. In those early days of sobriety, that gave her the detachment from him that she needed to stay calm and sober.

Carolyn was living with a violent, drinking alcoholic when she came into AA. She had come into the program before, many times, and listened when some people suggested she leave him—that he wasn't good for her sobriety. This was good enough advice on the surface, but she got drunk each time she left him. People just figured that she didn't have it in her to stay sober. Perhaps not; however, this last time she attended Al-Anon as well as AA. (She never missed an AA meeting, though; she just made sure she went to an AA meeting on the days she also went to Al-Anon.)

She had been abused all her life; she was so terribly dependent on men that she was, in early sobriety, unable to leave men *and* alcohol, too, without feeling as if she would just die inside. Al-Anon gave her that cushion—it taught her how to live in the same household as her spouse and still maintain her sobriety. She learned not to react to his "stuff." She learned she had the right to leave the room, leave the house, and go to a meeting. She is now five years sober.

Is it true that Al-Anon is just a place where they don't like alcoholics?

To *some* degree, many families in *early* recovery feel morally superior to alcoholics, and make no bones about it. Many alcoholics in early sobriety feel arrogant towards family members, and they make no bones about that, either.

When we hear recovered family members talk about "alcoholics invading our meetings," and when we hear recovered alcoholics talk about "outsiders" who come into *their* meetings as "earth people," we're not talking about just an alcoholic/family-member dilemma, but a human one.

Is there not an inverted snobbery, oftentimes, among people who boast that they don't read books? Do intellectuals often look down on those who own color television sets?

Don't we *all,* at times, puff ourselves up at others' expense?

But, can we who are trying to get well and not die from alcoholism, in *any* form, afford not to be honest with ourselves when we do this?

What wonderful things we can see when alcoholic and non-alcoholic family members begin to truly co-exist in Al-Alon.

When alcoholics begin to accept their spouses where they are (with their anger that masks *their* fear), the spouse's recovery speeds up tremendously. They can then let down their own defenses and begin, perhaps for the first time in their lives, to feel actually friendly towards an alcoholic. But this healing can only happen when they are accepted as they are, and alcoholics can only begin to accept them when they can momentarily step out of their skins and try to feel the pain that caused the anger. *Alcoholics can feel the family's pain empathetically only after they no longer feel guilty about pain they have caused. This is a terribly difficult task for alcoholics, perhaps more difficult than the spouse's task—but, oh, so healing for an alcoholic.*

And if non-alcoholic family members would try to catch themselves when they start to feel morally superior how different our lives would become.

Of course it makes one very angry to stop doing the things mentioned above! It's all we've had! For years, it looked like *he* had the fun, and all the spouse had was the "being good." And it *does* feel good to feel better than someone else.

Don't do it for the alcoholics, but when we give up that one last vestige of anger towards alcoholics, then, and only then, are we *really* free from alcoholism.

But this does *not* mean "putting up with his junk." It means, instead, giving *ourselves* permission not to put up with it so that we can't get *renewed* chronic resentments that hurt *us*.

But, if you are new in treatment for families, this is *no* time to be told to drop your anger. That would be playing into what you have been told: that you exaggerate and are crazy and wrong.

Letting go of anger can only happen *after* you have *detached yourself a lot and after you have* learned to stop allowing your alcoholic spouse to stop hurting you. That is the *only* appropriate time when *anyone* has the right to counsel you to drop your anger, *even for your own sake.*

For—even though dropping your anger is important for your health—*done too soon, its self-invalidating side effects* are more detrimental to your health than waiting a while until you are ready.

Write On:

Your feelings when it is suggested that you eventually let go of anger towards alcoholics, *given the above information.*

Suggested Activity:

Do *one* thing today that helps you to trust, to validate, yourself. (You might like to do one thing that you *know* you do not need advice about, but that you usually ask advice for.)

5

We Attach So Much Importance to What He Says and Does

I know a spouse is getting well when she starts to say, and means, "Who cares what he says any more?"

When we are so very sick, when we first come to treatment, we wonder about his every word—and we wonder about ours. We worry lest we say too much, or too little. We wonder if we are detaching ourselves "lovingly"; we feel like failures when we're too attached; then, we feel guilty when we feel *less* attached. If it's not guilt, then it's anger; then guilt; then worry when the guilt lessens!

We constantly take the *wrong* moral inventory of ourselves. We think this continual beating on ourselves, this constant self-analysis, is self-inventory.

Self-inventory is assessment of a situation in which we see what is effective and what is ineffective. What most spouses of alcoholics overlook is that their preoccupation with the alcoholic and how he feels or thinks is ineffective—and that a more healthy, "selfish" looking into what makes *her* happy is what gets us all well.

What happens when we spend so much time worrying if he meant what he said?

Janice told me her husband was always bugging her to get a tan. Before she went heartily to work on that (ignoring her own needs in order to spend hours in the sun—she tanned with difficulty), she worried herself terribly that she was inadequate in the summer when everyone else looked "good." When she got good and tan, and asked him about it (and she knew she looked good)—he murmured his approval with a slight shrug that said, "Who cares?"

And he didn't care! What she didn't realize was that he never *cared that much about it.*

Sandi had a similar experience with a haircut. *How many women married to alcoholic men have gotten haircuts that have turned the heads of other men on the way home, only to hear their husbands tell them, "You look masculine"?*

When this occurs in an alcoholic household, something terrible (in addition to all the other terrible things) happens: in a "normal" household, a woman can get a haircut, and her husband can dislike it, but his remark will probably not be soul-cutting. And her reaction will not take what he says to heart so much *because they don't have a* many-years-long history of bizarre, hidden attacks from an alcoholic—and expectations of those attacks, and scars, and unhealed bleeding.

So, even though five months later, when Sandi's husband is in a good mood and *means* it when he tells her that her haircut is "sexy," when he makes another crack about her in *another* area of her life, she is usually unable to "remember" his pattern of saying things that are very hurtful (and underneath it all, not even meaning them).

If we truly want to get well from this craziness, we must begin to allow ourselves to see that we live with a crazy person (or crazy people). And that we must not put it any other way. Otherwise, we think *we* are crazy. We need to keep telling ourselves what normal men do in similar situations.

Someone reading this chapter who never lived with alcoholism, might say, "Why a chapter on a tan and a haircut? After all, alcoholism is killing people! Is *this* all she worries about?"

These issues are the iceberg-tips that pop up as "issues" every other day or so. If they were isolated incidents, they *would* be petty. But, they are episodes in a chronic play of ego-erosion and crazy-making.

We ignore, we overlook, the larger issues that most women *leave* relationships over—issues that cause courtrooms to remove visiting privileges—issues that shock most people.

We just can't stand it when we've lived with so much and want just steady decency in return—and our souls are eroded, once again.

So what do we do?

First, when we are in a crisis, we have to remember to *stop,* and tell ourselves the *truth.* That truth is that when the alcoholic is saying he finds some part of our physical appearance offensive or unattractive, he is seizing upon a slender thread of something that he knows, instinctively, will cause us to be upset. *And it means no more than that to him.* He does *not* "believe" what he is saying. *He doesn't even care about what he is saying.* The particular point about your appearance is a side issue that is actually insignificant to him.

What is at issue for him is *power.*

The power to keep you jumping, afraid. The power to keep you so involved with your bruised ego that you turn to him for approval. You see, he needs to feel *powerful.*

If he can continue to feel powerful, even though underneath it all, he actually feels powerless (though he would never admit this to you), then he can continue to tell himself that he has himself under control, that he has you under control. *Illusion spreads.*

Meanwhile, what is *really* at issue for you is getting out from under the illusion that he is keeping you emotionally intact.

Only then do we begin to experience detachment. One of the powerful ways through which we achieve this end is to stop asking him what he thinks about how we look.

Another way is to laugh—even a forced laugh—when he volunteers the information that we look unattractive.

Another way is to wear shocking pink when he says that we look good only in black.

As a good friend of mine says, "The worst thing you can do is let an alcoholic know you are afraid of him."

Another area, a very hurtful one, that I'm often asked about is, "If he goes off with another woman, does he still love me?"

In 99 percent of cases, the answer is a qualified yes. Yes, in the sense that he loves you as much as he'll ever love anyone else besides the bottle.

Does he "love" her (the other woman)? She is probably one of two things: a drinking buddy or someone who does not *yet* complain about his drinking. Give her three weeks. I've had so many calls from women who told me how they were, at first, devastated by this other woman, only to be called by *her* later and begged to take back her husband. The other woman couldn't stand him any more than the wife could.

We forget. We think we are losing "Prince Charming." In reality, we've lost the frog.

Alcoholics, in the main, cannot keep up the illusion of "good guy" when living in close quarters with other people for more than three weeks. The alcoholic tires easily of the strain of pretense. He longs to and needs to drink the way he does. And, once he's that drunk again, no power on earth is going to be able to make him act like Mr. Nice Guy. If he was violent with you, he'll be violent with her. If he was unfaithful to you, he'll be unfaithful to her. He cannot change patterns as long as he continues to drink.

Will he get sober for her? He may make a half-hearted attempt at it, for a while, to "show you," but that "motivation" doesn't usually last long. If all drinking alcoholic husbands who left their wives, threatening to get sober for someone else, *did it,* there'd be a lot more sober people out there.

You don't have to feel guilty about hoping that won't happen. Of course, it would be "nicer" to wish him well, but if you don't, it's entirely under-standable. Besides, sobriety, like all other things in the world, is not a result of magical thinking on your part. He'll either get sober or not. It has nothing to do with you. Try not to think like the two-year-old who wished his daddy would die—and then when his father died, felt guilty for "causing it." Life doesn't work that way.

Back to the question of "does he still love me?" Do you remember seeing movies about heroin with-drawal? Remember the scenes where the actor would writhe in pain, sweating profusely? Can you imagine him caring, at that point, whether he loved his wife? Every time your husband needs a drink, he's going through withdrawal, and that means terrors (not just fears) and terrible physical things. He might not "show it" in a dramatic manner, but that is what's happening. And, when he's not going through withdrawal, he's planning on how to get the alcohol, and enough of it, for when he knows he'll go through it again. So, his life is *consumed* with thoughts of alcohol. And, it's *so* terrifying, and *so* consuming that he's annoyed and surprised that anyone should think he would be concerned with anything else. His whole life is *unconsciously* a play around the getting of enough alcohol. And that includes his choice of women. *He's protecting his supply when he chooses to go off with a woman "who understands." It's that simple.*

This overwhelming preoccupation with obtaining *more and more alcohol, and the denial of that preoccupation,* is the bizarreness he lives with. *You cannot fathom the depth of that preoccupation and the depth of the lying he will do to keep up his disease. As they say in AA, alcoholism is cunning, baffling and powerful. I am not exaggerating when I say that you probably do not have* any *idea how much he really revolved around alcohol, and that other women are truly a side issue.*

Write On:
Your *immediate* thoughts as you read this chapter.

Suggested Activity:
   Read this chapter, and what you just wrote, whenever you start to fear the other woman.

6

For the Man Involved
With a Woman Alcoholic

The very circumstance of living with a wife who is a drinking alcoholic is, in a sense, more devastating to a man than to a woman living with an alcoholic husband. If the alcoholic wife goes to bars to drink it is particularly fearsome, for everyone knows that it is not difficult for a woman to obtain drinks from other men, and this may have very little to do with actual physical attractiveness.

If she drinks solely at home, it has to be depressing for her husband to feel like he's hiding her, in a medieval sense, like a deranged relative in the house tower. "Why am I living like this?" he asks himself over and over—too guilty-feeling, too responsible-feeling, to let go.

A man named Jim told me of his longing aches when he saw other men going shopping with their wives. A normal thing to do. But he could no longer do that, because he did not know whether she'd want to stop for a drink. She had reached the point in her alcoholism where she couldn't stand up without help after she drank only two drinks. He couldn't bear the humiliation of other people's stares. "They don't stare like that at a wife in the case of a husband who has had a bit too much," he told me bitterly. "But they laugh at *me.*"

There was the day he overheard his neighbor call him "a poor bastard." Phil and John—friends from the neighborhood—had been discussing Alice, and his window was open enough to overhear their comments.

"You know, she's not half-bad-looking. Maybe she's one of those wild types!" Phil laughed.

John offered, "Yeah, maybe old Jimmie can't keep up!" Their laughter caused Jim to shut the window in embarrassment.

If a man drinks hard, it's assumed that he "plays hard," but no one assumes that there is necessarily a sexual problem involved. It is not assumed that he's philandering. And, if he is, no one sees his wife as a freak failure. (After all, "boys will be boys.") It is not so with women alcoholics.

Let's take a look at the Roman Catholic Church. The hierarchy has no trouble sending priests to treatment for their alcoholism. The hue and cry, however, over admitting that some nuns may be alcoholic is rampant. Why? The "brides of Christ" aren't permitted to be alcoholic; this simply can't be possible.

One almost cannot erase the unconscious thought in most people's minds that women alcoholics are loose women. It is mouthed that alcoholism is a disease—but it is *believed* that it is a shame. And I believe that at the heart of the stigma, for women, at least, is the sexual stigma that accompanies the usual "lack of will-power" myth.

Look at Hollywood films: a beautiful drinking heroine has no "self-control"; she sleeps with everybody; she repents; she *must be punished;* and if she lives to survive the punishment, she is a *good woman for the rest of her life.* The end.

What does this *do* to the husband?

The emotional turmoil that goes on within him must be terrible. He *knows,* even if he does not hear; he *knows* the whispers about him, about her. But only *he* knows his wife's terrible pain. Only *he* hears her beg him to help her when she is in withdrawal, when she has the unknown, terrible fears. He feels he *cannot* be tough and let go. Heaven help him if he deserts her. He would not want that to happen to anyone—to himself, to her, to a dog.

If he does not get help, in the form of going to Al-Anon, he cannot know that he can retain compassion, and still let go of helping her disease (the disease that begs him to help *her*)—let go of unwittingly helping her to die.

"It feels wrong, this letting go. *You don't let someone die!"* George told me, as he sat in my office.

"George, people in Al-Anon aren't going to tell you to do anything. They're not going to say that you *must* do *anything*. They're only going to welcome you, comfort you. They know your pain. They've felt that pain themselves. They're only going to tell you what happened in their homes—what they did that finally really helped. And they won't expect anything of you. As they say in Al-Anon, 'Take what you like and leave the rest.' Perhaps you can just take it one meeting at a time. If you don't like it, you don't have to go back. Or, try another meeting."

"Sometimes I want her to die," George went on. "Sometimes I want to walk out and never come back. I wish so bad I were married to a *conscious* woman! *Is that too much to ask for?"* he screamed, sobbing openly. As his crying subsided, he asked me, "Am I nuts? Do you have contempt for me?"

I was barely avoiding crying myself, much less having the feelings he thought I must have—the feelings he believed the world held toward him. The pain in that family—in her, in him, in the children—was terrible.

When you go from extreme to extreme, it is very tiring, very emotionally draining, very depressing, immobilizing.

She plucks on your innermost fears when she threatens to leave you if you stop "helping her." Your *mind* tells you, "That's her disease talking," but you are terrified nonetheless.

She yells that she'll get someone else to help her, to live with her. Your rational mind tells you, "Who'd put up with it?" But she, her disease, convinces you temporarily that her alcoholic behavior, her so-called "sexual abandon" while drinking, can lead to a wild, wonderful roller coaster of a romance, even if it doesn't last. You can't stand the thought.

We need a bubble-bursting technique. We need to remember that *every day* the disease is progressing. And what alcoholic is attractive, except to another foggy alcoholic? And, even then, what alcoholic is attractive to another alcoholic for more than a few hours?

Al-Anon will help you to stop being prisoner to that threat—that implicit threat of other men. It will help you to stop living under the gun, to get sick and tired of the threats of a sick person. *After all, what are you being threatened about? Is your life in danger? Are you in danger of losing the most wonderful, most admired, most attractive woman on earth? She is threatening that she, an alcoholic who is committed to drinking, would, if you stopped supporting her drug habit, leave you for another drunken person.*

It is all an illusion.
Alcoholism is built on illusions. It cannot exist without crazy-making illusions. If a woman alcoholic screams at you, "I'll find someone else if you don't help me," *she is not talking sex, she is talking panic.*

Women are taught to get a man *"to take care of them."* They are not taught to get a man for sex. If a man screams, "I'll get someone else," he *may* be talking sex. But if a female drinking alcoholic, in the throes of panic and withdrawal, is threatening you with someone else, she is telling you that she will find someone else to "supply" her with her narcotic—her pain remover—her alcohol. *The last thing in the world she wants is sex. She just wants relief from the pain of alcohol withdrawal. And she wants reassurance from you that she will always have an abundant supply. That's all she wants.* And usually she only threatens you with this leave-taking when you let her know that you are at the end of your rope concerning her behavior around alcohol (which she rightfully interprets as meaning that you will eventually decide to stop her supply).

Her threat of "other men," therefore is only a "red herring." *The issue* is alcohol craving; the issue is alcoholism, pure and simple.

Let me repeat: *Alcoholism cannot exist without your believing crazy-making illusions.*

And the main illusion we are talking about, particularly for the man living with a woman alcoholic, is her so-called *exaggerated* sexual attractiveness because she is a woman alcoholic. We believe at one and the same time she is beyond anyone calling her attractive, yet we believe there is a primeval attractiveness, a primeval sexuality, about being a woman alcoholic. *And that is all illusion.*

Alcoholism is *not* about sexuality; it is about *pain*. It is about craving alcohol. It is about existing around that drug. It is about living under anesthesia while awake.

Another "normal" man would not find your wife attractive.

Al-Anon will help you rid yourself of the terrible fear that another alcoholic will carry her off. Al-Anon *will help you not to care about that, any more.* Living under that burdensome fear, that terror, is like living in prison.

And no human being should have to live that way.

Al-Anon will gently, ever so gently, erase that fear; it will do it so easily that you will not notice—until it is gone.

There is a fear that everyone feels—the fear of being left. We all know that fear; all people who are abandoned know that fear. But alcoholic family members know that fear more than anyone, because after years of living with an alcoholic, one's self-esteem is so eradicated that one believes that he or she is a small, insignificant person. You actually feel smaller than you are; your drinking alcoholic partner looks and looms larger. Therefore, you feel less able to live alone than reality warrants. *However, you are an adult person who lived alone before, and can choose to do so again. It is all an illusion that she is keeping you intact.*

Al-Alon will gradually help you to build up your self-esteem.

It will take away that gnawing, terrible guilt of abandoning her.

It will help you to stop going from extreme emotion to extreme emotion, twenty times a day.

It will help you to get to, and stay in, that middle ground called dignity.

It will help you to help her, if you choose to.

If will help you, despite yourself.

Write On:

One of the illusions you may be believing, concerning your "responsibility" for your wife's continued maintenance, while *she* continues to drink and/or take pills.

Suggested Activity:
   Do one, small, very-little-time-consuming activity (one that is pleasurable), an activity that allows you to believe more strongly that you could live alone, if you had to (and with less pain than you anticipate). (Example: Hire someone to do a chore that must be done, but is something that you dislike doing.)

7

If You're Bored by Nice Men, or If You're "Just Going With" an Alcoholic

I've received many calls from women who tell me they are married to men who still have very deep problems even after they have been sober for a couple of years. Many of the man have frequent rages. Very often the husband will tell the wife, after he has unsuccessfully visited six or more therapists, *"You* find us a therapist that works then!"

I usually recommend a good internist and perhaps a neurological specialist to examine her husband. This will determine if his problem is at all physical. If it is not physical, and if her husband is truly *willing* to let go of blaming the world for his problems, is truly *willing* to believe in, *and act upon,* the "spiritual axiom" that AA talks about (i.e., "When one is troubled, the trouble lies within"), then much of the rage will subside when he remembers to be willing.

During the first three to five years of sobriety one is not really "out of the woods." One is still through a protracted withdrawal syndrome. Alcohol is still leaving the body, and the body's hormonal systems and brain centers are constantly readjusting, and this creates a chronic stress. At the same time, it heightens the intensity of one's feelings. Add to this the fact that your husband is only one or two years old in terms of learning to cope with raw feelings while being stone-cold sober.

This does not excuse anything.

However, if he acknowledges that *he* has the problem, and is *willing* to take full responsibility for his feelings and actions towards others, hope abounds.

First of all, he can get himself a good, tough, male AA sponsor who believes in marriage in the old-fashioned sense—that a man is responsible for the tender care of his spouse. This sponsor will "call" him when he starts to blame you and justify his childish rages. This sponsor will teach him *how* to pray. (This involves simply letting the alcoholic know that when the rage takes over—if he truly dislikes it—he can ask his Higher Power to fill his heart with peace.)

All too often the statement, "Get me a therapist that works," is a ploy. *When that one "doesn't work"—he will say it is her fault.*

I usually wind up the conversation in such a case by suggesting that if there is nothing wrong physically, the wife should tell her husband to find his own therapist by praying about it, and if he is truly willing, the answer will come.

63

What does all this have to do with the chapter title: "If You're Bored by Nice Men or If You're 'Just Going With' an Alcoholic"?

That kind of statement is usually made by adult children of alcoholics. This means they were reared in a home that was full of bizarre, deep-seated patterns like those described in the previous case: one is manipulated into feeling responsible for another person, and one is constantly kept on the go with excited misery.

An alcoholic fills a very great depth of need for the spouse who was reared in an alcoholic home. The emotional heights are oh, so wonderful, and the pain is so excruciating—just like it was in the home where the spouse grew up. It is the only kind of acute pain that fits *exactly* into the tiny holes *and* the craters that still exist after one leaves home. Those "holes" are like a vacuum; they abhor being empty.

Alcoholics fill those "holes in the soul."

I believe that knowing this is very helpful, for it *exposes* much of the so-called "mystery," bringing the reasons for bizarre behavior and feelings to light. It is a jolting reminder that this is not fun, but illness.

And we don't want to hear that. Not really.

I've told clients that alcoholism is an addiction, not *"chemistry between us"*—and I've instructed them not to use the term "chemistry" so they can stop romancing this sick relationship.

If an alcoholic who is not yet ready to stop drinking goes to a counselor, and that counselor confronts him about his drinking, the alcoholic will often terminate the counseling relationship. Alternatively, the alcoholic will frequently seek another counselor who will simply talk about "communication skills."

Years later, however, that same alcoholic may remember what the first counselor said, and if that alcoholic is in enough pain, and is willing to surrender to help, he may remember—and believe—and act upon it.

In the same vein, if you are reluctant to give up the "pleasure" of thinking along the lines of "chemistry" instead of "addiction," try putting the "chemistry" idea on the shelf, at least temporarily, in order to see how the "new point of view" changes things.

There are some real antidotes for combating this aspect of the family illness of alcoholism:

(1) Keep open to learning the patterns of adult children of alcoholics, especially in the area of choosing partners. It is painful, *and it takes away the "fun," but try to think the "fun" through.* Look at your mother. And your father. You'll *see* your "exciting" man five years down the pike. You'll see yourself—terrified, seething with rage, feeling trapped. It doesn't take long for the honeymoon to end. And *no* one is really capable of prolonging that first flush. That's just the natural order of things.

What may now be only pebbles *will* become boulders, I promise you. So, if you can't say "no"—try, at least not to commit yourself any more than you are at present. Do *some* holding back. Give yourself time to get past the honeymoon stage *without a firm commitment*. And don't worry—no matter what he threatens, he'll wait. As Al-Anon says, "It's hard to lose an alcoholic." Once you learn the truth of this, it's a valuable, lifetime lesson.

(2) Do specific things to slow yourself down in other areas. If you are the oldest child in your family, you learned to overachieve, believing you are responsible for everyone. If you are the youngest, you are clever and funny. Another pattern is seen in the way you start projects and have difficulty finishing just one before going on to another. You are *constantly* berating yourself for "not finishing."

Try this: choose *one* project. Do it slowly. Finish it. You will feel relieved and proud of yourself, but, at the same time, you will feel uneasy. What does one fill the void with? Don't worry; time spent acting "regular" instead of "frantic and overachieving" will eventually change your self-concept and you will get used to being content. This "slowing down" of the racing thoughts and actions will build your self-esteem. And anything that builds self-esteem, from this *inner* place (not from externals, because these don't do it) will contribute, in time, to your not choosing alcoholics.

(3) See a therapist who is a specialist in behaviorial therapy, and who will work with you on this area of your life. List the positive attributes and the self-destructive patterns of your non-alcoholic and alcoholic parents. List similar ones of yours. List those that are "double-edged" swords (i.e., responsibility: it can be both helpful and not helpful to be responsible, depending on when, with whom, and how much). See the things you want to change. Work on them, *in small pieces*.

Try not to counter-compensate by going all the way to the other extreme to avoid a trait you dislike. This can be just as debilitating as the original trait in your parent's life. (For example, I know one woman whose mother used frantic housecleaning as a diversion because her husband was a difficult alcoholic; the daughter, now grown, never cleans.)

(4) Give yourself *time*. *Remind* yourself that this attitude of "I want it all *today*" is a typical alcoholic family pattern. Remind yourself, also, that this feeling robs you of *enjoying* the present moment. Try to enjoy today. It will be difficult at first. You may be able to enjoy yourself, in the present, for only three minutes at first. Don't worry. It will get longer. (We would blow our circuits if we got it all at once.) Our bodies need time to adjust to change. The normal life pattern doesn't want everything to happen at once, right now, always, and forever. That's our frantic approach to life.

(5) Try biofeedback and relaxation techniques in order to learn to *slow down*. It's insidious, this "racingness" we feel. *It keeps us sick. It keeps us in excited misery. It keeps us choosing sickly, excited people.*

Write On:

1. Do you really want to marry this alcoholic man, or do you really just want to be married? Do you feel driven by this *at all?* No one will read this, if you prefer they don't, so be honest.

2. Are you willing to give up the *edges* of your pain, if not the whole, excited package?

Suggested Activity:

1. Tell yourself at least three times today that what you have between you and your alcoholic partner is a lot less "chemistry" and a lot more "addiction."

2. If you do not choose to tell yourself the above, allow yourself to put it on the shelf for a future time.

8

If You're a Helping Professional Who Has Clients Who Are Both Alcoholics *and* Spouses of Alcoholics

This client usually has special fears, the main one being the worry that an unhealable schism will develop between him or her and the still-drinking spouse. This is not an unfounded concern. And it cannot be waved away with a simple admonition to "Just don't think about him while you're here in treatment." Many clients go "AWOL" when they hear this.

I find that if I do not identify and treat this problem *at once,* the chances of losing this client to alcoholism are much greater.

I identify the problem by being very direct. In my first sessions with the client, I question him or her about the drinking pattern of the spouse. If there appears there *might* be a problem, there usually *is.* (Alcoholics, new in treatment and "foggy," are not

72

adept at spotting another's alcohol problem unless it is as pronounced as their own.)

I find out if that client drank *with* the partner. If not, I seek to determine if they did share some "good times" around drinking. Does the client say he or she wants to leave the relationship? Is this an "I am strong" false front, an impulsive statement, or is this person, right now, ready to leave permanently? (The latter is usually less frequent than one might imagine.) If he or she balks at answering "yes," when asked if he or she would like to start divorce proceedings right now—then proceed on the assumption that the ties are still very strong. Any other assumption, despite bravado on the client's part, underestimates the "pull" the relationship still has—a "pull" that is often destructive to sobriety, and therefore *cannot* be ignored.

At this point, I would be very open with the client and let her or him know that you *understand* and you do not desire to put down the very real fears she or he might have. Discuss each fear at length, preferably in group *and* in individual sessions. Stress that no one is expected to "be strong," and not have feelings of terror, jealousy and abandonment.

Some of the other common concerns this person may have are:

1. Fear that the still-drinking alcoholic will leave.
2. Fear that the client can no longer be in bars, making sure the partner doesn't "pick up" someone else.

3. Fear of returning to the home, because of the booze there. Fear of *not* returning to the home, because of the possible loss of his or her partner.
4. Fear of a lack of communication. "What do we talk about, if I'm sober?"
5. Fear of a terribly "alone" feeling, once he or she is back at home.
6. If the client is very emotionally dependent at this time, even if he or she knows the spouse wouldn't abandon him or her, the fear that the client will be displeasing to the drinking partner can be extremely terrifying.
7. Fear of you (the counselor) "putting her down" if you realize how very dependent and child-like she is at this time; and fear that you will demand that she makes steps toward independence that she knows she is unable to carry out right now.
8. Worry about loss of financial support if there is a separation, and possibly property loss, especially if the client is a woman with small children, or married for many years, without any job skills.
9. Fear that the counselor will put tremendous pressure on her or him to leave the home situation; and fear of withdrawal of the counselor's support if the client is not emotionally able to do so.

Let's talk about these fears, and possible ways to deal with them effectively.

First, I suggest that you identify which clients you have that may fall into this category of alcoholics with drinking alcoholic spouses. Treatment centers sometimes ask the spouse not to drink for a specified time while the client is in treatment. If, however, the spouse is an alcoholic, he or she usually cannot comply with this request. It's a good idea to go the route of asking the spouse to "give up drinking" for that time, because it certainly helps to crack through the denial that "He hasn't got a problem." If it's only the word of the client, the spouse can continue to further deny it. If the treatment center sets the goal of abstinence, however, and if the spouse cannot stop drinking during this set time (and if all the other spouses are abstinent), this takes the onus off the client to "prove" her spouse is alcoholic, too, causing the spouse's alcoholism to stand out "like a sore thumb."

Immediately, I would arrange for that client to go to Al-Anon meetings on a regular basis, in addition to her AA meetings. This is not to take the place of AA meetings, but is in addition to them. (When she leaves treatment, I would encourage her to attend Al-Anon where there may be a beginner's AA meeting preceding it.)

She will need Al-Anon twice a week, at least, at the beginning. She needs to get right into Al-Anon by getting phone numbers of old timers whom she can call when she feels panicky. *This program can do more to calm her down around the question of her spouse than anything an alcoholism counselor can say to her, unless that alcoholism counselor is also, or was also, the spouse of a drinking alcoholic, and lived through those fears, too.* Even if you are in that category, I would still send her to Al-Anon, because the feedback from all those people in that meeting will reinforce her in a way that no one person possibly can.

Al-Anon will let her know, over and over again, that the spouse is not as powerful as she has been led to believe—that "It is hard to lose an alcoholic." (He'll come and go, and come and go, for fifty years, if you let him.) She will hear the stories, first-hand, of women and men who *were* as terrified as she is, and who are not frightened any longer of losing an alcoholic spouse.

I would combine this powerful, constant reassurance of Al-Anon with the alcohol-education knowledge she's getting at the treatment center, stressing how during this protracted withdrawal time her emotions will be heightened about *anything*. It is important to give her the hope that she will not feel this strongly about him given a few months. It doesn't take long to get *some* peace—that will happen very shortly. But, the alcohol and/or pills need gradual time to get out of the system. Each week, she will feel better, stronger, more independent—and that is irrespective of anything she does, as long as she stays sober.

She will not feel as threatened as regards her husband, if she stays sober. She *will* feel as strong and independent as all those women she wished she was like, if she stays sober. *That's a promise.* It is the alcohol and pills that *make* one cling, that *make* one not let go of terrifying, dependent feelings, that *make* one trade off one's self-respect in return for caretaking.

She will no longer feel threatened by abandonment if she stays sober. And what she will learn is that once she stops being afraid of losing him, he will pick this up (as alcoholics have their own special "radar"), and much of his game-playing will stop. It is no longer "fun," if you don't have a victim.

She will stop fearing a lack of communication because she will learn that much of the "communication" was destructive and caretaking in nature. She will no longer need that. She will learn that, in normal homes, there is more silence than she is used to, and she will learn to love it.

She will learn through AA, you, and Al-Anon that she need never be alone again; she will learn that she was never alone, in feeling alone; that all of the forty million alcoholics in the country felt alone in a crowd and felt that we never fit in.

She will learn (not right now, because she is too new to grasp this) that if she stays sober, and goes to AA meetings, she will get such inner strength from a power outside of herself that she will, probably for the first time in her life, learn to trust her gut. So, if someone ever does demand that she do things she is not yet ready to do, even if they are things that are "good for her"—she can say "no" without guilt and fear, but with dignity.

And, as AA promises, she will begin to lose her fear of financial insecurity. That will no longer be held over her again. Life will get into perspective, and inner peace will become much more important.

Write On:

Write a list of Al-Anon contacts who are both gentle and patient, who may be called upon to help clients in this situation.

Suggested Activities:

1. If you have never been to Al-Anon, and if you are a helping professional, attend four or five "open to the public" meetings, so that you can get more tools of comfort to use with clients who are still involved with drinking alcoholics.

2. Start a special kind of group in your treatment center: An institutional Al-Anon group for newly sober clients who are also related to drinking alcoholics that they are concerned about. Ask Al-Anon to come, on a regular basis, to lead this meeting.

9

Dealing With Your Alcoholic Child When Your Spouse Also Has a Drinking Problem

Most people who have an alcohol- or other drug-addicted child also have a spouse who is an alcoholic. It is an inherited, generational disease.

What I often see in my counseling practice is a couple who come to me about their son who is an alcoholic. The dialogue that takes place in the first session or two usually follows this pattern: The father (who has an alcohol problem, too, but undetected by the wife) says, "She's too hard on him."

When I ask what that means, he replies, "Oh, she 'sees it' everywhere. I mean, I can understand when she doesn't like the trouble he gets into. I really come down on him for that, too. He's got to learn to control his drinking! It's better than it used to be. He stopped all that pot. Now, he just drinks. But he doesn't seem to act normal about it. In a way, however, you can't blame him for going out and getting drunk now and then; after all, his mother nags him all the time about *any* drinking! She's such a fanatic!"

Many times I am not the first counselor they've sought out. They've been to clergy who see her role as just someone who, "if she loved them enough," could make everything all right. They've been to psychologists who "want to get to the root of the problem," and talk about "the family's communication problem."

The counselors have been so sophisticated (except in the area of alcoholism) that they are "against alcohol abuse" but do not realize the extent of the disease; they have no idea how many people *are* alcoholics. Usually, this counselor also does not recognize the symptoms of early-stage alcoholism. So, the counselor becomes the unwitting partner in collusion with the diseased spouse, thus adding to the non-alcoholic parent's feeling of despair and insanity.

If the teen-aged son acts out *his* alcoholism more than his father does, the alcoholic father's disease remains hidden even more. He can point to the son "who *really* has a problem."

On the other hand, the non-alcoholic parent's efforts to help the son seek help for sobriety are thwarted by the father who certainly doesn't want a *no*-drinking rule in the house! Thus, he constantly tells his wife to "cool it" and to "stop nagging!"

She knows what the answer is, but the seemingly rational obstacles her husband places in her path are confusing. The professionals' muddying up of the issue with *their* lack of knowledge often makes the non-alcoholic parent give up trying to get help. She's just tired of being told she is "overreactive."

These factors give all the more reason why she needs Al-Anon to help end her isolation, to see that other parents—millions of them—have gone through the same situation. She will find answers and strength there. She will get reinforced that she is *not* crazy when she is called that at home by both alcoholics. There, she will learn to stop her own denial, when she does not want to face the fact that her husband, too, is an alcoholic.

She will stop wanting to deny his alcoholism, no longer afraid to face it. She will learn how devastating it is to deny it. Denial of reality has a way of permeating our very beings, and makes us mistrust what we know is true about our entire world. It makes us fear making *any* choices, any decisions. It makes us regress and become fearfuly dependent.

Al-Anon will also take away the guilt that all parents with addicted children feel. And parents who themselves are adult children of alcoholics invariably have unresolved, irrational guilt left over from their childhood (when they felt, unconsciously, that they had to "fix" everything for everybody to make "it" all right for that family to go on. And when they failed at that, as all children must, of course, the guilt was terrible). Imagine what happens when the parent adds to that the guilt of having a child with the same problem, and not really believing it is a disease, but a problem related to "child-raising."

Adult children of alcoholics are masters at beating themselves with irrational guilt.

Al-Anon will help them to understand that they cannot truly cause, cure, or control another's alcoholism.

By itself, prayer, even though wonderful, does not provide all the answers. One needs to go to a group where people with similar problems are present in order to stop feeling that it is a moral problem, in order to stop feeling like you are the only one in the world with this problem, in order to learn to truly "turn it over" to your Higher Power.

Adult children of alcoholics who are spouses and/or parents of alcoholics not only have trouble with irrational guilt, but also have problems with trusting a Higher Power. *Truly* trusting. We often cling to our old ideas, and they are unconsciously based on how we felt about our parents. If your mother was punitive, you see God that way. If your father was a drinking alcoholic, you may see your Higher Power as incompetent, and someone who needs you to keep after Him to make sure He finishes the job and does it well.

Persons who live with alcoholism for years, especially persons who themselves were born into it, and never lived in households without active alcoholism, have terribly exaggerated feelings. They are often not aware that their feelings are so much more intense than those of others. "Normal" feelings become "terrible."

So, when you do what *anyone* would do, in normal circumstances, when you didn't know what to do with an alcoholic child—when you helped, as any normal mother would, you felt guilty when that did not work. When you felt all the things that the family members of this disease feel—obsession, worry, terror—you felt guilty that your *feelings* did not make it all right. ("If I worry so much, and care so much, why isn't it helping?") You blamed yourself when you couldn't help; and when you first went to Al-Anon, and learned to detach yourself, and not feel guilty, you felt guilty when you didn't feel guilty, for not "being down there with him, hurting with him, commiserating with him." Alcoholism, the family disease, did not allow you to win, either way.

Add all this to the "normal" guilt parents feel. I've never met a parent who didn't feel irrationally guilty at times for the things that happened to their children, for the things that no one could have controlled. Add the guilt of alcoholism to this, and you have an immobilizing, debilitating, over-whelming concern that must be turned over to treatment if you are to function normally again and learn to *really* help your child.

One of the ways through which parents beat themselves up is to ask themselves, over and over, *"Did I do my best?"*

Of course you didn't do your best all of the time! No one does! No one is perfect.

We have a relatively short life on earth. Our reason for being here is to live life to good purpose. Guilt holds no good purpose. Its only function (other than as a warning sign, when the guilt is rational, to change behavior) is to keep us feeling immobilized so that we are not of best use to others, or ourselves.

Write On:

The last three times when you felt overwhelming guilt, how long it lasted, what it did to you physically and emotionally, and whether it accomplished any good purpose.

Suggested Activity:

Allow yourself to stop beating yourself, just for today, and to attend an Al-Anon meeting. Usually there are both daytime and evening meetings, and if you have young children, you can take them along (bring coloring books, crayons, and other books). It's free, lasts only one hour, and will bring *days* of relief. (If you still don't want to go—*go anyway*. Your family disease is telling you not to go.)

10

From "Pity to Punish"

We've all done it.

We, who are alcoholic-family members, whether or not we are also alcoholics, have acted out this syndrome more than most folks do.

How does "from pity to punish to pity to punish, and back again" operate?

Carol, who travels a great deal, and attends Al-Anon meetings wherever she goes, was in a Texas town where it was announced that the group was going to a detox center at a local hospital, to bring an "institution meeting" to the patients. (That is, a meeting where a few members of Al-Anon lead a program at an institution as an introduction to what Al-Anon is all about and how it can help.)

She and other members spoke with ten family members in a conference room off the main hall in the alcoholism ward. Two nurses from the ward also attended. It was very clear that one of the nurses disliked the female family members.

Her face was as tight as a drum whenever one of them spoke; she looked as if she were a walking thundercloud. When she was called out into the hall to work with an alcoholic patient for a few minutes, Carol watched her. She acted out such anger towards the alcoholics; then, when any of them was cowed, she dropped the anger and went into pity. When she came back into the room, she again expressed much rage. Called out again, she had an encounter with a newly sober alcoholic who did not respond well, apparently, to her pity, and she turned on him also. This scenario went on throughout the half hour before the meeting, during the hour of the meeting and for forty-five minutes afterwards.

Carol reported, "I seem like such a snoop! But I was fascinated. It was like watching an unconscious quick-change artist. She had no idea of what she was feeling, it seemed. She obviously had no idea that she was so transparent!

"What was going through my head, off and on, and kept me watching, was: am I like that? Do I have such ambivalent feelings toward alcoholics, and perhaps family members too, that I don't even know it?"

Often, the non-alcoholic daughter of a female alcoholic has trouble acknowledging, and resolving, her hostility towards non-alcoholic, female spouses of alcoholics. She is the most likely to drop out of Al-Anon, being "surrounded" by the people she fears, and dislikes, the most. If she stays in treatment, she often gets into a terrible power play (in her head, mostly) with those women. Most of them are not aware of the machinations of this manifestation of the family disease, and either treat her with kindness—or, if they are particularly sensitive to hostility aimed at them, give her "a wide berth."

If she wants to get well more than she wants to stay angry, she will eventually drop this, and get on with her program. Fortunately, many choose this course.

Cassie is a recovered alcoholic woman, happily married, sober seven years. She is twenty-eight years old, a remarkably successful executive. Until the unexpected baby was born, she had her priorities in order, and her life seemed peaceful.

She had been the youngest child in an alcoholic family. She had no prior life experience to draw on for taking care of children. She had just thought of them as "adorable."

When Cassie was a toddler herself, she was abused by two alcoholic parents. When she got older, she felt she was the only child of her parents to "care" about them. In fact, the other children acknowledged their anger towards their abusive parents, and kept out of their way. Cassie felt she had to help them. She prayed for them; she became the parent herself. She made dresses for her mother. She had a part-time job, but she saved enough every week to take her mother to the movies and to eat out.

She felt very good about being able to make her mother a little bit happier. Her mother, otherwise, was often bitter towards her father, and felt she had had a bad life. She often told Cassie that she "worked her fingers to the bone" taking care of her. She also let Cassie know that she had been an unplanned child. Cassie didn't show her hurt. She went into the bathroom and cried quietly, so her mother wouldn't know. In a strange way, the hurt and the crying felt a little good. She didn't know why. It comforted her, as her mother never had. It let her tell herself, for that short time, "There, there, that's all right, Cassie."

It also led to a lifelong habit, until she got sober, of not letting people know how badly she hurt inside, for fear that they would either make fun of her or tell her, as her mother did when she cried when she was abused: "You keep on crying, and I'll *really* give you something to cry about!"

Cassie had her baby.

The feelings went like this: "Isn't he *precious?*"; "I can't *stand* the crying and the taking care of it!" (when the baby was a little older); "I *can't* say no to a little baby! I can't stand the guilt! He *cries!*"

The baby learned nothing about boundaries or limits on his behavior. He did anything he pleased— making Cassie very angry. So she yelled at him. And frightened him. And felt guilty. And reindulged him. And again he knew no limits, and acted out. And she got angry again. And yelled again. And remorsed again. Etcetera.

92

Cassie was exhausted and wanted, at times, to give the baby away. She felt guilty about the thought. More remorse. And the continuous cycle occurred over and over.

She went to Al-Anon, and it took her a while, but she started to see that she was *re*acting, not acting as an adult mother, but as the child who was so afraid of not pleasing that she would get "punished" by the child either not loving her, or more than that, by the child being emotionally so hurt that Cassie could not stand the anguish of watching this.

What finally got through to Cassie? She literally "watched" one of her sponsors in Al-Anon— a woman who was truly one of the nicest human beings she'd ever met. She wished this woman had been her own mother. Her sponsor was raising her grandchildren in her home. She was one of those old-fashioned child-raisers who was "stern but very loving," which meant she knew how, without even a *thought* of guilt, to raise children with love and how to say "no" when necessary.

Cassie decided that this was a case of applying a principle she had learned in treatment: Make believe and you will believe. Get the body there and the mind will follow. Act like an adult and you will become one. After several weeks of pretending she was like this woman, and saying the things and doing the things (despite guilt) that this woman would do, she eventually found herself being guilt-free for three days, and setting the limits that she knew would be good for her child.

Sam worked with John at a high-pressure job.

John was the type of alcoholic who never said anything snide to you, straight on. He'd just "make cracks" at you all day, and when you called him on it, he'd say, "What's wrong with you? Can't you take a joke?"

Sam found himself not saying anything to John when he did this, but it built up inside him, until he exploded with anger, yelling at him, over and over. Afterwards, the next day, when John would be very quiet, and hurt and looking like a hangdog, Sam would feel a sense of disquiet. He didn't know it was guilt, but he acted on it.

He went out of his way to try to be very nice to John. John would "sense" that Sam felt guilty; John would "play" on that guilt, acting out again with his snide remarks.

Sam, after having been "so nice" to John, felt hurt, betrayed. He kept it inside again, not saying anything. The snideness built up; Sam exploded, followed by remorse, and so on.

If you are identifying with any of these scenarios (or remembering a scene similar to any of these), you are not alone. You are one of more than forty million alcoholic-family members plagued by this particularly painful aspect of family alcoholism.

94

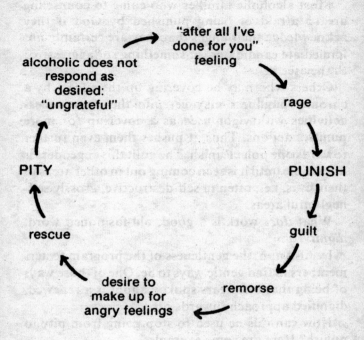

"after all I've done for you" feeling

rage

PUNISH

guilt

remorse

desire to make up for angry feelings

rescue

PITY

alcoholic does not respond as desired: "ungrateful"

First, let's deal with what often *doesn't* work in counseling people from alcoholic families: assertiveness training.

Most alcoholic families who come to counseling are so afraid of being punished by God if they acknowledge their anger that they are certainly not immediate candidates for something so "aggressive" as they see it.

Others who may be covering up their fears by a chronic toughness may get into the assertiveness activities with vigor used as a cover-up for more punitive actions. Thus, it pushes them even further towards one pole: Punish. The guilt this engenders is not visible until it is seen coming out in other areas of their lives, i.e., often in self-destructive, grossly self-neglectful areas.

What *does* work is a good, old-fashioned word: *dignity*.

In Al-Anon, the gentleness of the program fosters members to find gentle ways to be. One of those ways of being that one hears spoken about is a renewed, dignified approach towards others.

How can this be used to stop going from pity to punish? Here are some examples.

Stephanie had to meet with her attorney from time to time. He had a great need to control others, feeling so out of control of himself. He manifested this by screaming at her, and "summoning" her like a servant, when they were to meet. (They often had to meet in public places because of their busy schedules.)

She would enter the lobby, looking around for him. He would very obviously snap his fingers at her to come to him. What Stephanie would do, before, was to *run* to his side, afraid of displeasing him. She came to counseling, afraid to "tell him off." We suggested she not do this, as it was too uncomfortable for her. We suggested, alternatively, that she do whatever came to mind, after she first thought of the word "dignity."

She was thrilled. She came back to the next session, having been through it again with him, this time as a different person. "I thought of dignity, and when he summoned, I just walked slowly to him, with my head up. I felt such a pull, it was hard. And I was scared. It was like disobeying a parent. And when I got to him, we just looked at each other for a second or two, and I knew that he knew that all the intimidation was over. He tried once more, by yelling at me a little, but I told him that I didn't want him to speak to me in that way. I just thought about the way some of my sponsors in Al-Anon would say it—the ones who were thirty years older than me, and very dignified. And I just responded in the same tone that they would use."

Families of alcoholics need *permission* from a terrible internal sense of guilt towards the world to stop taking stuff from sick people. The use of dignity is a necessary stepping stone for those who are afraid to immediately shed guilt, and express anger. And that's most of us.

The use of dignity goes further than that. There is such a calm about the word and, therefore, a calm in its use, that there is no thin line to walk to avoid getting into aggressive, punitive behavior, as there is when one is trying to be "assertive without being aggressive."

Write On:

Describe an area of your life (family, work, friends, acquaintances) that involves the painful-to-you, pity-to-punish syndrome.

Suggested Activity:
The next time you are goaded into anger by a person who chronically does this to you, say to yourself, *"Dignity,"* and see the difference in your response.

11

Why Do I Have to Go to Al-Anon? I *Know* What to Do Now!

When I have a client who expresses the sentiments of the chapter title, invariably the common thread running through all our talks is *guilt*.

"I did so much for him!" or "After I thought I was being so nice to him, going out of my way for him, he _____, again. What did I *do*?" or "I've been divorced for three years now, and I don't need Al-Anon" or "Yes, I do have trouble saying *no*. To everyone, actually. When a guy sits next to me on a bus, and he's bothering me, I *can't* tell him to leave." Or "My husband died of alcoholism five years ago. Why should I go to Al-Anon? I keep wondering if I should have done an intervention. Maybe I should have. Was I wrong?"

"*Was* I wrong? *Am* I wrong? I am guilty. I deserve to be punished by God. Therefore, I'll punish myself, first, so that He might see I did punish myself, so maybe *that'll* stave off the wrath of God. And if I keep beating myself all the time, maybe I can keep *real* punishment at bay. And if I stop beating myself with guilt, what will I do with the stillness? It's anxiety-provoking."

You can't have active alcoholism without drinking. And you can't have an active family disease without guilt.

Guilt is the mainstay of the family disease. It keeps us sicker than any other manifestation of alcoholism.

How does regular attendance at Al-Anon combat that guilt? You go to a meeting. Other people tell how, that week, they were able to stop doing such-and-such that they had never been able to stop doing before. (One of the many ways they've learned to say "no" to the disease.) You see that person, sitting there, smiling and happy. He or she is not being "zapped" by God, not being punished. You see that person return, feeling better, doing better, week after week, even though he or she keeps saying "no." You see this same phenomenon in ten other people, twenty other people, repeatedly, at each meeting. The repetition "tells" you that *it is okay to say "no" to the disease and not feel guilty, not feel that you will be punished. It happened to the others, and it can happen to you. You, too, can get well.*

We do not learn well from head knowledge. We learn better from people, for God speaks through people. And, we need repetition—actually, we need reinforcement. This is because, in our daily lives, the disease of alcoholism is getting reinforced. We may be divorced from the alcoholic; he may be dead, but our patterns, our habits, live on. They live on in the form of low self-esteem, in not being able to say "no," even to sick *strangers*.

There's a vicious circle that occurs between guilt, low self-esteem, and crazy-making.

We are "battered" when we "take it"; we lose self-esteem; when we get angry, we feel crazy because we are told that it was our fault we were battered; when we get that beginning of a shadow of a doubt about our sanity, the alcoholic knows this (he has "radar") and homes in on our self-doubt, attempting to increase it.

In more subtle forms, this occurs with anyone with whom we are feeling desperate about keeping our relationship (if they are sick in the mirror-image way that we are sick). In other words, if the hooking-process "works" with this person, he or she will sense that we will do anything to keep or get their love. They will start this all-too-familiar game with us, the same game we played with the alcoholic five years ago before he died.

The patterns live on.

Even if you never speak up in Al-Anon, even if you do nothing but attend meetings, and get phone numbers of others whom you can call and allow to care for you when you need them—even if you do nothing else, Al-Anon will heal these areas in you.

And you are not unique.

That healing has happened to hundreds of thousands of families. Keep coming back, and it will heal you. That is a definite promise.

Write On:

The exact reasons why you may not want to go to Al-Anon.

Suggested Activity:

Ignore those "reasons" and remind yourself that *that* is your disease talking—the same one that tells the alcoholic that he "doesn't need" AA, and that he "can do it himself."

12

More on Detachment

"*This* time, it went like this . . ." Sheila started to tell me. "I had stayed out late, after a family recovery meeting, and he got frightened. Oh, he didn't *say* he was frightened. Not him! He never admits to vulnerability. I mean, if that were *me,* I'd be saying, 'Oh, please comfort me! I'm so scared that you stayed out late!'

"No, he just acted angry. And told me that he was 'irritable' because he was sleepy. Then he asked me if I went out to eat with the girls after the meeting. And his eyes looked real scared.

"I wanted to comfort him, but I knew I couldn't. I knew that if I gave him what *I* would have wanted— upfront reassurance that I wasn't doing anything wrong—he would've started a fight. I just answered him. He stayed frightened, angry, and went upstairs. So, I went upstairs, too, and told him why I had talked after the meeting—how I was uptight and needed a 'meeting after the meeting' and how I had been crying and upset. This should have let him know that there was nothing for him to be afraid of. He acted like it was all okay. And then the 'zinger' came; he made one of his cruel remarks.

"I just backed off and went downstairs.

"At first, I wanted to blame myself. 'If I hadn't stayed out, if I had only been more sensitive,' etc.

"But I knew that that wasn't the case. First, he's made cruel remarks before and they were never precipitated by me. Second, he's only scared because I stayed out an hour later. Last year, I stayed out of the house after meetings a lot, because I couldn't stand his mouth. When I've told him about 'first cause,' he just gets angry. That's his answer to everything. Nothing's wrong with *his* behavior. *I* just imagine all hurts. If he says anything cruel, it's all okay, because 'it's not deliberate.'

"I've been through this merry-go-round too often. Nothing gets changed if I yell. If I reason, if I'm calm, if I do nothing, if I leave, nothing ever changes.

"I went through, and past, the phase of expecting him to change. Then I went through the phase (and still am going through it, but less) of being angry with myself for staying, *knowing* that *he's* not going to change.

"I've gotten used to the fact that I *will* be able to get out of this situation emotionally, some day. I'm just becoming more aware that if I try, one day at a time, to work my program—that is, to be gentle with myself, to have fun with myself and friends, to broaden my world—I will be letting this program wash on over me.

"Then, I went through the phase (and this one lasted a long time) where I knew I couldn't change him, but I thought I *had* to let him know how angry I was. It was a little bit of 'not letting him get away with it'—but it was mostly, 'I've got to get it out, or I'll scream inside for days!'

"I wasn't getting anywhere with getting any peace.

"I reached a little bit of a bottom. I wanted to *detach*. I wanted not to yell, discuss, or say *anything* of any importance any more to him, so that he would have less power over me. One of the ways I had given him power to determine how I would feel emotionally, was to run to him when things were good, and when things were bad. He would be my protector from outside intrusions; he would be my wonderful support; the one who was so proud of me.

"I didn't want to pay that price any more.

"I knew I was willing to give up (some, anyway) of what I thought was the most priceless part of our relationship: the fact that he was proud of my achievements. When I did well at work, he would let me know.

"Then, I got somewhat depressed thinking of giving that up. I knew that there had to be a middle ground of growth. I could, as Al-Anon says, *"take what you like and leave the rest."* They say that about what is said in meetings, but why not apply it to my marriage?

"I decided to make his approval less important by spreading out my getting-approval base from others. My sponsor already was approving. I decided to get one, two, or three closer friends. I decided to make that a goal. We would be supportive of each other's achievements. I would seek out women who were of shared interests.

"That way I'd *need* him less. I figured that if I *needed* him less when things were good, I'd also need him less, period.

"I also decided that a lot of my obsession with him was habit. And habits, with persistence, can be broken, and replaced. I would write down my areas of 'hooking' and slowly replace those needs with other people.

"I felt totally helpless over being able to give up that defect of character: my dependence on my spouse, emotionally. But I had read that although will power doesn't work where we are defenseless, God does give us power, when we use our will power, to achieve what He wants for us. And I knew that God did want me to stop using this human as a tin god.

"So, He would give me the power to carry that out. I figured He'd give me the power in His time, and if I used it properly—with dignity—where I could.

"I also read that psychiatrists were more willing to look at a patient's belief system before they judged him to be ill. I knew that depressives were being taught to change their belief systems, in order to stop feeling depressed about a situation.

"I knew that my program taught me to change my reaction to an event. But, I believe that it is easier to change my reaction to an event when I *think about* that event in a different way. In other words, when I change my belief—my premises—about the situation.

"I decided to try to get some detachment—some *distance*—from my alcoholic, by seeing him in a truer light. I believe that I have been believing some very erroneous things about him and me. I think I am very symbiotic—I *attach* so strongly, with no apparent reason, and very quickly.

"And yet, that attachment is so replaceable.

"I've had *just* as strong a sick attachment to *every* other alcoholic male I've gone with. And I *didn't* have that strong an attachment when I've gone with a 'normal' male. And that *attachment* is what has been familiar, has been comforting. *It's not the man, it's the attachment that I crave.* The man has just been the embodiment of that attachment.

"It's like walking up to a relative stranger who fits the mold and saying, 'Here I am. I'll curl up in a fetal ball. Please hold me, forever. Please tell me, over and over, that you love me. I'll do anything for you in return. I will take care of you; just make sure that you keep telling me, and that *I* keep telling me, that *you* are taking care of *me*. And I don't care how nuts this sounds. Because that's not what's important.

111

What's important is that you *stay* with me. Forever and ever. And ever and ever.

"And I have been terrified of the possible absence of that.

"I have felt that my inner being would possibly be forever depressed if I did not have that in my life, as my center.

"What in the world would I replace it with? And, *could I?* Would I *ever* be that well? I don't have that much belief that I will be well enough to handle the absence of 'that.' My belief also tells me that I am sub-sick.

"Now that I have written down this muck, I can almost see it physically. This 'thing' seems almost tangible. It is a large, white, shot-with-red, bloody thing. It dwells in me, although it is not attached in any real way to my body. It seems to live in a self-protective sac—and yet it seems, now, quite puncturable.

"It might be a bit of a bloody mess when it is punctured, but a lot less than I thought it would be.

"I believe the process has already started."

"I know that detachment can seem plodding, heavy. It can seem like a chore. Almost impossible, at times. It can add to my depression, weigh me down.

"But it doesn't have to be that way.

"That's the hard way to go.

"It can be three thousand times easier—*and*

faster—if I go the route of 'being good to myself and having fun.'

"I have seen it work in others. And I want what they have. I have seen some persons plod through detachment, and they are a glum lot. I have seen others determinedly go out and have *fun* when their homes were madhouses.

"And I'd rather go that route."

Sheila works at a job, buys clothes, gets her nails done, goes on vacations, accepts that there will be guilt (better *that* than depression), goes out to eat, goes to concerts, plays, and films. She has the same amount of detachment that Zelda has, only Zelda chooses a grimmer path.

Sheila knows that "sickies" will go on being sick. She just chooses to be watching a movie when they are being crazy. I really think it's easier that way.

Write On:

How it feels, emotionally, and physically, when you think about how you would feel if your alcoholic spouse left. Then describe how it would feel two weeks later. And then, two months later. And then, one year later.

See how you *know* you would feel better.

Suggested Activity:

Call a person you've met of your same sex who is "your kind of person." Arrange to meet this person and investigate whether you'd both enjoy a friendship.

Talk to more people than you do about "outside things and events."

Think of other ways in which to expand your life, since it has been so contracted by alcoholism.

13

The Alcoholic Is
So Very Predictable

No, it doesn't take the hurt out of it, entirely. Not by a long shot. But knowing that the junk coming out of the mouth is so very, very much a part of the pattern of eighty million other alcoholics in the world does help a little.

It helps to make him or her not so powerful. It makes dealing with this person easier, makes this alcoholic-cut-out-of-a-typical-mold-just-like-from-a-cookie-cutter, easier to see through. It makes it easier to tell oneself that, "I may not be able to detach myself from all your junk today, but I will someday, because even though you and I are telling me that you are so very powerful—it's just your disease that is so powerful. If *you* were the powerful one, you wouldn't even *have* it, and you wouldn't need to continually try to prove to me that you are so powerful.

"All this I may not be able to use for going into detachment immediately, but it's being put on the shelf, into my positive unconscious, I am getting 'weller.' "

And, if you say that to yourself, you *are* detaching—just by saying it. No, not all at once. But a little part of you is detaching—is *seeing*. Is observing. Is at a clinical distance. And that is detachment. Ah, you say, it is detachment of sorts, *but*—

That "but" is our disease talking.

When we cannot do it all at once, and yesterday, we think we have made no progress. I really believe, in my own life, that if I got everything as fast as I think I want it—as I think I even may need it—it would fall flat on its face. I think that if it happened that way, I would unconsciously not cherish it as much; I would not trust it as much. I would turn my dissatisfaction to other matters, immediately upon getting what I want, when I want it, whenever I wanted it.

This is *not* to say, "Don't worry about the detachment part of it; if you had it, you'd be just as obsessed by something else." It is just that healing is, of necessity, often slow. And that makes it no less a miracle when it happens.

This reflection about the progression of detachment, healing, is yet another way to get more calm into one's life, for it is only in reflection of one's *own* growth, its bits and pieces, that one becomes sure-footed that one *is* getting well. And there is not one person who keeps going back to recovering groups of families—who tries to practice the program—who does not get well.

This knowledge, this *sureness,* this promise of recovery—this seeing the progress—is calm-making, and therefore, gives one more detachment. Even if we are powerless over the alcoholic, over the disease— the program of Al-Anon give us the power to transcend it.

In the process of seeing more of the pattern, I am reminded of a "Grapevine" (monthly magazine of Alcoholics Anonymous) article. A recovered alcoholic told, how, in his first months of sobriety, his grandiosity told him that he was "getting too well" for his wife. She, in Al-Anon, saw the pattern being just somewhat different from his flaky drinking behavior, and did not panic. She merely suggested that they put a rope down the middle of the house, and live separately on either side of it, since it was cheaper than supporting two households. He agreed. He lasted three days—since she told him, also, that they could not speak to each other, since they were supposed to be in separate households!

Needless to say, he begged her to abandon the idea.

Expect early-sobriety insanity. I would take the suggestions of a newly sober person as seriously as I would take the suggestions of a drinking alcoholic. It takes eighteen to thirty-six months to clear the body of alcohol (that is the length of the protracted withdrawal syndrome). During that time, one can except unknown fears, tremendous anger without sufficient basis for it, and many of the crazies that occurred during drinking. And, in between bouts of this there will be periods of lucidity. Which makes for crazy-making. You begin to trust, and the pins get knocked out from under you. But, in sobriety, the periods of lucidity get longer and the crazy times get shorter.

This is part of the pattern of alcoholism—the cookie-cutter effect. *Knowing* it helps to not be as surprised by it. Not being as surprised by it—being angry about it—nonetheless constitutes a form of detachment.

What's the answer? Not reacting gives both of you *time*. If he doesn't get a reaction, the air will be let out of the sails, so to speak. Your marriage will have more time to survive. And that *time* factor is a healing one for him. The less you react, the more he'll have to reflect on his behavior, since he can't drink, to ignore it. This doesn't mean you don't feel anger!

I would just give him a wide berth during his first year or so of sobriety. A good friend of mine even "left" her recovering alcoholic. She took the children and skedaddled back to her parents, telling him she wasn't going through his first year with him, that she'd had enough from the drinking! She told him she loved him, and that she'd call him, and he could call her, but she'd had *enough* of his problem! He's been sober twenty years, now, and they are happily back together.

Another predictable pattern may occur:

After you confront him (calmly, and only once) about his drinking, he will go through a period of weeks, or months, in which he'll seem to control his drinking, and make you think you erred in your judgment—that he *doesn't have* a drinking problem!

As they say in AA, *"Alcoholism is cunning, baffling, and powerful."* They also say that *it is patient.* And an alcoholic who is not yet in the final, deteriorative stages of alcoholism *can* still control his or her drinking, off and on. And that *is* confusing. Once more, you are told you "are overreacting," or "are a fanatic," or you "see it everywhere!"

They say in AA that if the mention of God drives people out of AA, the booze will drive them back in again—if they're lucky.

Remember that *you* are powerless over his disease. And, if you fall for his con-game that, "If you didn't nag so much . . . ," you will believe that somehow, you caused his drinking again. Baloney. You can stand on your head, do everything wrong in your life, and if he wants to stay sober, he will. Conversely, you can do everything right, and if he wants to be drunk, he will.

Remembering the patterns, the scripts, the cookie-cutter effect, the *sameness* of alcoholics, can take off some of the edge of the pain that's been inflicted upon you.

And all the "figuring out," all the analyzing in the world, all the trying to determine "what will make him happy," so that he will stop doing whatever hurtful thing he's doing, *nothing* will work so well as just closing your eyes to him, reminding yourself that it's just more of the same pattern, the same script eighty million other alcoholics are acting out tonight. Just go out and have yourself some fun.

Write On:

Write out the last two times (in a script form) when he tried to make you feel crazy.

Suggested Activity:

"Coldly" determine how not to react. If he gives you "that look," when you suspect it's coming, don't have eye contact with him. When you speak with him, look just beyond him. He loses his power over you, that way. *You* become your own person, and he loses his power to fuse your insides to his.

SECTION TWO
The 350 Secondary
Diseases/Disorders to Alcoholism

Acknowledgments

This section has been made possible by the invaluable help given to me by the following:

William (Bill) E. Barr, Sr., C.A.C.

LeClair Bissell, M.D. Past President, American Medical Society on Alcoholism; author, *Alcoholism in the Professions* (Oxford University Press); internationally renowned authority/lecturer.

Edward J. Kitlowski, M.D. Impaired Physicians Committee of the State of Maryland.

James R. Milam, Ph.D. Worldwide authority and lecturer on alcoholism; pioneer in the treatment of alcoholism as a disease; author, *Under the Influence* (Bantam); co-founder of the Milam Recovery Center, for alcoholics and their families, in Bothell, Washington.

Richard (Dick) Prodey, C.A.C. Alcoholism Program Coordinator, The Sheppard and Enoch Pratt Hospital, Baltimore, Maryland; lecturer on alcoholism.

Charles Whitfield, M.D. Internationally known author and lecturer on alcoholism; author, *Alcoholism and Spirituality* (Resource Group); co-founder of the Resource Group, Baltimore, Maryland, a treatment for alcohol, other drugs, and family problems.

Introduction

by LeClair Bissell, M.D.
Past President, American Medical Society
on Alcoholism; author
Alcoholism in the Professions

When anyone visits a physician, questions may be asked about the use of alcohol, tobacco and other drugs. All too often the heavy drinker as well as the alcoholic will minimize the amount of drinking and will not initiate a discussion of problems that alcohol may be causing. The usual pattern is that doctors fail to probe, patients evade but don't actually lie and the full story is not revealed. The drinker doesn't want to be scolded or told to abstain and the busy physician neither wishes to be seen as a scold nor to get involved in what may be seen as a social rather than a medical problem.

Alcoholism is called a disease of denial. Not only does this denial blind the drinker to what is happening, but friends, family and physician all too often are equally unseeing. Ours is still a culture that

129

is reluctant to criticize drinking or to diagnose alcoholism until the slaughter on the highways reaches massive proportions or until an individual is so deteriorated that death is imminent or the skid-row stereotype is achieved.

When doctor and patient are working together to discover the cause of an illness, both often fail to consider that alcohol may be a major contributor. Both may be reluctant even to consider this possibility because both have serious misconceptions about what alcoholism is and what can and should be done about it.

Most medical schools do a good job of teaching students about the toxic effects of alcohol on the body. They lecture on the changes in physiology that it causes. They usually describe accurately the process of physical dependency on alcohol and, when this is extreme, how to treat the withdrawal states that result from the abrupt cessation of drinking.

What medical schools fail to do is to prepare the students to look for the more subtle manifestations of an early drinking problem. Questions aren't asked or aren't asked skillfully. Clues are missed. Vital information is not obtained or isn't used. A diagnosis is made but it is often incomplete if not actually wrong. *Symptoms are treated as if they were primary illnesses* or attributed to other causes.

If the real problem is alcohol, the symptoms are likely to continue as long as the drinking continues. If the drinking stops and permanent physical damage has not yet occurred, time and abstinence often lead to complete recovery. If there really is an illness independent of the drinking, very often a serious problem will become a relatively minor one or one that can be managed much more easily.

Certain illnesses are so commonly associated with heavy drinking that almost everyone, doctor and layman alike, is aware of the connection. Cirrhosis of the liver and pancreatitis are almost as likely to make us ask if drinking is involved as is the report of a single-vehicle accident at midnight on a Friday. There are other common illnesses that also go hand in hand with drinking but where the connection has been missed. In my own experience, the most common diagnoses in adult alcoholics which prove to be directly attributable to their drinking are "essential hypertension," "adult onset diabetes" and "idiopathic epilepsy." For an enormous number of patients, these problems vanish when the drinking stops. For many others they don't, but often the need to take medicine ends.

Obviously alcoholism doesn't protect anyone against the other illnesses, physical and emotional, that afflict the rest of humanity. It certainly can make matters a lot worse and in many instances can prevent treatment from having much useful effect. If combined with a variety of drugs, it can alter their action or effectiveness. This applies to prescriptions for both physical and psychological problems. Even when psychotherapy is undertaken with complete sincerity by a patient and that with a first-class therapist, if a drinking problem is allowed to continue, the treatment almost always fails. It may seem impossible that someone could see a mental health professional on a weekly or more frequent basis for a period of months or years without an alcoholism problem being detected but this was common in the recent past and still occurs all too often.

What to do? Reproaching the medical profession is not enough. We do have to improve our teaching and hopefully we will, but that will not be soon enough to reach many of those colleagues who graduated years ago and are currently overwhelmed with other demands on their time. There is simply too much material, too much that is new and changing, for many of us to keep up. Drug addiction and alcoholism are usually not high on the average doctor's priority list. They should be but they're not.

The would-be patient can wait for a new generation of better-trained professionals to emerge from the schools of medicine, nursing, social work, and psychology, but if there's a problem now, that's not soon enough. Since we can't trust the professional to be well-informed, it may be left to the patient and the concerned family to question whether or not a problem exists in its own right or whether alcohol is at the root of it. The cart may indeed be before the horse and the bad situation used to explain the reason for drinking may in fact be caused by the drinking itself. Frequently the best way to sort this out is to stop drinking altogether, refrain from substituting other mood-altering drugs for alcohol, and see if the problem clears up. *If this seems an impossible task, that may be yet another reason to wonder if a dependency on alcohol has crept into one's life.* Is drinking too important? Underneath all the rationalization, is the truth that one can't stop? (Note that the ability to stop drinking altogether is common to many alcoholics who nevertheless find that they are unable when they do drink to predict the amount they will drink or to keep promises about drinking that they have made to themselves.)

If one is alcoholic, the situation today is much more encouraging than it was in the past. Treatment is more widely available and much better than it used to be. Alcoholics Anonymous is available almost everywhere and one can visit their "open" meetings without any confession of a problem or commitment of any kind. Many communities have local councils on alcoholism listed in the yellow pages that can direct traffic to competent treatment resources. (That usually means people and places with special skill and training in working with people suspecting trouble with alcohol and with other drugs as well.) Usually the worst thing to do is to do nothing at all and to hope that things will get better all by themselves.

It used to be that medical students were taught that there were two diseases, syphilis and tuberculosis, that could be called "the great masqueraders." This meant that almost any symptom in almost any part of a patient's body might very likely turn out to be caused by one of these two. We were to consider both of them as possibilities before we settled on another explanation for what was wrong. It didn't matter that the patient was a minister's wife, a company president, a migrant worker or even a colleague. Diseases are no respecters of persons. Since today antibiotics have made both of these old enemies less common, one could make a case that today's greatest masquerader is now alcoholism. It must be considered before it can be faced.

Foreword

by James R. Milam, Ph.D.
Co-founder of the Milam Recovery Center
in Bothell, Washington; author,
Under the Influence

Organs and systems malfunction for various reasons. Alcoholism may be one, if not the exclusive, reason when they do. Often, it's one of the major factors.

Most diseases have borderline stages as well as full-blown manifestations. Alcoholism very often is the one factor that pushes a "tendency" to have the disease over the edge into a full-blown manifestation.

Epilepsy is one example. Many people are borderline epileptics. Under normal circumstances, they never manifest the disease. But, during even *mild* alcoholic withdrawal, a borderline patient may go over the edge. Many patients on Dylantin in active alcoholism never need it after sobriety.

Virtually all the other diseases have borderline degrees, except when alcoholism pushes them over.

I am asked, "What if I take vitamins? Can I stop or ward off the effects of alcoholism?"

The effects of alcoholic drinking are so powerful—one is in such a chronic toxic state—it cancels benefits of proper vitamins, jogging, and nutrition. A very watchful-of-his-diet alcoholic just slightly slows the deterioration.

It's not what gets into your gut that counts; it's what gets into your bloodstream. Your liver, etc., is constantly fighting to survive the chronic toxic attacks. Also, the cells cannot properly process their own waste materials, and they, therefore, are awash in their own toxins. Nutritional supplements have a *very* slight effect on this.

Early researchers studied skid-row alcoholics and found malnutrition. They thought it was due to their poor diets. But, as private patients became available for study, they found the same results.

Alcoholism seriously interferes with *every* stage of absorption, conversion, and utilization of nutritional materials.

So, the entire body is really toxic *and* malnourished—therefore, it is less able to ward off these diseases. The liver swells, to try to contain the toxins, so that they don't spread to the rest of the body. The liver is the major organ that has the job of controlling and converting toxins to waste materials. A liver that is *that* polluted doesn't have the capacity to do much else, i.e., its normal work, in getting rid of toxins, in warding off diseases.

Author's Preface

As one can see, after reading the preceding introductions and following interview, there is much to be included in future medical schools' and other professional schools' curricula on alcoholism.

One would only hope that in all future courses for helping professionals, it would be stressed that, 1.) alcoholism is often the *primary* disease and that these *secondary* diseases are caused by, or exacerbated by, the alcoholism.

And one would hope that professionals would be educated to explain to their patients that, 2.) many of these secondary diseases would probably not again occur, or at least be greatly diminished, if they stopped drinking.

And, 3.) if professionals, especially physicians, would realize what Dr. Bissell said is true—that "essential hypertension" and "adult onset diabetes" and "idiopathic epilepsy" are commonly due to alcoholism—and if they would tell their patients that one fact, just as outlined, tens of millions of lives could be saved.

It is so hard to tell a patient—no, to *confront* a patient—that he has alcoholism. Even physicians, because they are human, see it not as a diagnosis, but as an accusation.

The Good News

Alcoholics are often told (and wisely so) when they are in treatment facilities to wait—to *not* have immediate drastic treatment for non-life-threatening problems when they are newly sober.

Why? Very often, after six months to a year or two of sobriety, these problems disappear altogether or are greatly diminished merely because their causative factor (drinking) has been stopped.

Norman is a recovered alcoholic. He gleefully told me that he had his eyes checked just after he left the treatment facility. He had been one month sober, then. They said at the eye doctor's office that he needed very strong glasses. He told them he wanted cheap frames, "Because I'll need a lot less powerful prescription in six months!" They were mystified; how did he know that? He was told, in treatment, that most alcoholics' eyes get better in six months. In fact, Norman now has much better vision than he ever did when drinking.

Karel told me that when he drank, he had serious seizure problems. He went to many doctors, endured many frightening tests, to find out "the cause."

When they asked him about his drinking, he always told them he drank "a couple." He never said how big the "couple" were. When he stopped drinking, the seizures stopped. (How many costly and unnecessary tests could be avoided if one were honest with the doctor about one's drinking?)

John had the worst case of "dry eyes" that one of the best eye clinics in the country ever saw, said its chief of staff. Surgery was recommended as the only relief. After his third year of sobriety, John's "splinter" feeling in his eyes stopped; after his fourth year of sobriety, his eyes began to tear.

These stories are not exaggerated; they are not uncommon; they are not the work of people who want to "prove miracles." They are just the natural, physiological results of having stayed sober. (After all, if you stop hitting your head against a wall, your head will probably stop bleeding.)

14

Interview with
Richard (Dick) Prodey

Dick Prodey, C.A.C., is the Alcoholism Program Coordinator at the Sheppard and Enoch Pratt Hospital in Baltimore, Maryland.

Q.   What about alcoholics who read the following list? What about their skeptical questions such as, "I know eight people [even if they don't] who have these diseases. And *none* of them are alcoholics"?

A.   I think what an alcoholic might be doing, in saying this, is trying to repress feelings of fear he has about what may be happening to him. It's so integral to the alcoholic's system of denial to be able to say a couple of things: one is, "This doesn't apply to me. It may be true, but it doesn't apply to me"; the second is to make those who confront him seem ridiculous. He might say, "Yeah, but there are a thousand explanations why you could have a swollen liver and a swollen belly, and feel depressed."

He is trying to question the credentials, the authority, of the person who is confronting him—who is trying to get him to look at the *disease*—because he [the alcoholic] doesn't want him to do that. So, what he'll do is try to make enemies out of those who try to confront, or those who try to help.

He can do that by making those people seem ridiculous. You'll hear, for instance, those people who will talk about AA in ridiculing terms. And, that, in my opinion, is a denial system in full force, to separate the alcoholic from those who can help him.

His denial system needs to work *to keep him away* from people who will confront him with the fact that he *has* the disease and who will help him to recover from it.

His disease wants to keep the drug going—so, he can do that by ridiculing his potential help.

The alcoholic will, typically, so overgeneralize his own problems, so as not to have them.

The alcoholic will say, "Though this list is generally true for most of the population, I'm an exception. I'm different."

There are two words that kill alcoholics: "I'm different."

The alcoholic will ridicule the list, will ridicule the person who is presenting it. Or, he will try to remove himself from it by overgeneralizing it, most commonly by saying, "Everybody I know drinks the way I drink."

If everybody on the face of the earth drinks the way the patient drinks, then the patient's drinking is not of the universe he knows. If you can say that something is true for everyone, then it couldn't be a problem because it is "normal."

That's denial at work.

If the denial system can make a list of symptoms appear to be normal for most of the human race, it is essentially saying, "Your list is meaningless, because what is normal for the human race cannot be problematic for any one person."

Q. He goes back home and he surrounds himself, as if he had on a cloak, with his drinking buddies, and *that's* what he means by "the human race all have the same symptoms," therefore, it is "normal"; therefore, he does not have a problem. And he is *not* abnormal among his peers; they are *all* dying from alcoholism.

A. Sure. There's a two-headed denial in most alcoholics. It works either to ally him with people who drink and think the way he drinks and thinks, or to ridicule those who are different. And I think that that's what is in operation when the patient says, "You're a fool for presenting me this list of 350 items. Everyone I know has some of these problems, because I've already allied with people who make me feel normal about myself." That's denial at work.

Q.   What do you say, Dick, when you have an alcoholic patient sitting in your office who tells you, "Well, you gotta die from *something!*"

A.   I tell him that we're not talking about anyone dying from anything. We're talking about what you're dying from. That's isolation of effect. That's saying, "I desperately do not want to feel. If I feel any pain about this, I would do something about it. So, I will repress feelings that I could actually die from this; I will try to keep this at an emotional distance from me."

Q.   What do you say to the person who admits they have a problem, but who is too terrified to give up drinking or pill-taking? They think it holds them together, emotionally.

A.   I would say, "In your mind, it has become your glue. It has become the solution to your problem rather than its cause. *That* is what is perpetuating your continued drinking. The reason you feel you are coming apart *is the drug*.

It is *not* what is holding you together. And you won't know that until you are successfully abstinent and see that you can function better without it.

Q.   What about the person who says, "I don't believe you when you say that. When I take it, it calms me down"?

A.   Sure, short-term. It is perceived as the solution. But, what it solves is solved only short-term. In the long run, it *worsens* the very thing it appears to solve.

Q. How does it make it worse?

A. It is agitating the nervous system. Alcohol has only two effects on human tissue. It sedates, and it irritates. There is a short-term sedative effect, as long as you're drinking it. After just a few hours of sleep, the sedative effect of the drug, alcohol, will have worn off. It is followed by a longer-lasting, irritant effect.

Q. Does the same thing happen with the minor tranquilizers that affect the same brain receptors as alcohol?

A. It looks like it works the same way, yes.

Q. What do you say to the patient, who, when he first enters inpatient treatment, says to you, "I can't go through my anxiety without my sedation"?

A. I would say, "The anxiety you are experiencing is the anxiety of withdrawal. That what you are experiencing are all of the emotions augmented through a nervous system that is now experiencing the agitation of withdrawal. You need to stay abstinent from the drug to allow that to calm down."

If you remain totally abstinent from alcohol and drugs, and also work a recovery program, you will be better off than you ever were before. I have never seen anyone who has not felt better emotionally, and physically.

The cycle of addiction is always to create or to intensify problems and anxiety, so that the drug is perceived as the solution rather than the cause.

You know, when you talk about early recovery, you are really asking the question, "What is the nature of the disease that you are recovering from?"

And the nature of that disease is that it has caused both perceptual and cognitive distortions. So, one of the things that you are recovering from is the way in which alcohol has affected your thinking—your perception of reality—your perception of yourself, in that reality. And because it is a disease of denial, you don't even know your perception has been "off" until you are sober, and your perception has improved!

You have been perceiving the world, and yourself, through the fog of alcohol. What you need to recover from is that mental fog, *even though you think you are thinking normally.*

In active addiction, most people think they are thinking normally. They may function relatively well at their jobs and think, "There is nothing wrong with me."

If I spend twenty years doing some fancy rationalizations in order to perpetuate my addiction, *and do that unconsciously,* my thinking has learned to be aiming in the direction of exceptions to rules, rather than rules. Many alcoholics end up knowing more what they don't believe in, rather than what they do believe in.

They cannot tell you very much about what they believe; they can just tell you all about the people and situations they disagree with. This is not all alcoholics, just many of them.

We get into the habit of finding the exception to the rule, the excuse; how to minimize. The disease will force you to learn how to rationalize in order to perpetuate your use of the drug.

In addition, there are so many emotional problems that alcoholism causes. Such anger, or in others, such anxiety. Researchers at Harvard are now studying the brain and the effects of alcohol on it to determine why, in one person, such anger occurs, and in others, such fears occur.

Q. Why do you think that many mental-health professionals keep using the tack of "getting to the root of the problem" rather than insisting that their clients *first* stop drinking?

A. It is difficult to believe that a problem that has so recently been called a disease, *is* a disease. It is difficult to accept that, at least at first. Also, what you see are symptoms.

And symptoms sure do look psychological.

But, alcoholism only has three ways to show symptoms. The only way you can show that you have any symptoms of alcoholism are, 1.) medical— there are health signs that something is wrong;

2.) social—it is interfering with your abilities to perform your social roles; and, 3.) psychological—it shows up in terms of psychiatric symptoms: mood problems, emotional problems, distortions in thinking, etc.

So, it is pretty obvious. If the patient has neither social symptoms (a weekend in jail or family disturbances), or has not shown, yet, any health symptoms (withdrawal symptoms or swollen liver symptoms), then, what the patient reports to you are all psychological symptoms, especially in the early stages of alcoholism.

And so, you quite naturally assume that if there are psychological symptoms, there is a psychological cause.

The second necessary ingredient in that process is not the doctor's, it is the patient's. Many alcoholics would prefer to be diagnosed as having a psychological problem rather than an alcohol problem, either because it is more acceptable or because they cannot stand the idea of the drug being taken away from them, because their addiction has become so strong.

So, you have a physician who finds it difficult to believe that alcoholism is a disease, and you have a patient who only manifests, at that point, psychological symptoms; and you have a physician who has no training in how to confront it.

The doctor feels personally awkward in trying to confront it because he feels it is outside of his own realm.

And then you have the patient who does not see his drinking as a problem, who is in the thick of denial.

The patient is actually, unconsciously, *defending his drinking,* preventing the doctor from seeing it, and is perpetuating the very thinking that doctor has got going.

Q.   The patient says, "I drink a couple." A couple what? How big is each? And how often, in truth? It's minimizing.

A.   If you could just get all professionals to take detailed drinking histories, they could see that they are asking about *symptoms,* that they are not *prying.* That this is a medical disease, a mental problem. That it is not a moral issue.

As long as they perceive it as a moral problem or as a symptom of a psychological problem, the medical doctor, especially, will feel that he is out of his element.

He will feel that he is butting into foreign territory.

But, of course, twelve professionals can diagnose your alcoholism, your addiction; but, if you don't diagnose yourself as having the disease . . . in other words, my diagnosis is possible, but your self-diagnosis is critical.

Comments From a Recovering Family Member (spouse and mother of alcoholics)

"When I first heard about these secondary diseases—someone came to our meeting, as a guest, and told us about them—it angered me because it made me very scared. At the same time the program (of recovery) is telling you 'It's *his* problem,' you are confronted with the *depth of the reality* of the disease. It broke through my denial.

"When you're able to act, you do whatever *you* need to do, that you were afraid to do. It's a gradual thing, though.

"But, this list helps, because you're being told facts. *My* dilemma was, 'What do you do with the facts?'

"Eventually, I came to believe that the drinking was unacceptable behavior—*for me*. Many people told me, 'Don't dwell on his drinking.' That's true, but by getting into my own life, I came to a time when I did find that his drinking was unacceptable. Where before, I thought I had to put up with it, because it's an illness."

The list of diseases in the following chapters is by no means complete. When the disease's name is rather technical, as in most cases, a layman's description is provided. These definitions are not meant to fully explain the disease.

This section, *The 350 Secondary Diseases/ Disorders to Alcoholism,* is also available separately in pamphlet form. Ordering information follows page 193.

15

Chronic Neuropsychiatric Disorders

A. Generalized Neuropsychiatric Deterioration (Alcoholic Dementia or Chronic Organic Brain Syndrome)

B. Personality alterations:
   1. Mood swings
   2. Anxiety
   3. Irritability
   4. Increased impulsivity
   5. Aggressive outbursts
   6. Increased emotionality
   7. Grandiosity
   8. Unreasonable resentment
   9. Remorse
   10. Self-pity
   11. Suicide attempts
   12. Diminished sexual drive
   13. Pathological jealousy

14. Inability to think clearly
15. Obsessional and undefinable fears
16. Somatic (body) complaints
17. Psychomotor inhibition (slowed-down thinking process)

C. Withdrawal Symptoms:
  1. Agitation
  2. Insomnia
  3. Tremulousness (shakiness)
  4. Seizures
  5. Alcoholic hallucinosis (seeing and/or hearing things that aren't there)
  6. Delirium Tremens (D.T.'s: final stage of withdrawal; severe disorientation and purposeless overactivity with great stress on cardiovascular system)

D. Malnutrition:
  1. Wernicke-Korsakoff Syndrome (i.e., Acute Organic Brain Syndrome or "Wet Brain": including confusion, eye problems, and staggering). The effects of alcoholism on the high-brain centers include: disorientation, amnesia, loss of hand function, hallucinations, difficulty in thinking and walking, and difficulty focusing while seeing.
  2. Pellagra (a B-vitamin deficiency that shows up in inflamed skin, a rough, scaly skin on the

hands and/or the face; the inside of the mouth is swollen, red and inflamed; dementia and diarrhea)

3. Deficiency Amblyopia (dimness of vision as a result of alcohol poisoning)

4. Central Pontive Myelinosis (erratic and uncontrolled twitching; difficulty in walking and speaking; interference with all muscle functions)

5. Marchiafava-Bignamini Disease (progressive intellectual deterioration; emotional disturbances; confusion; tremors); occurs especially in middle-aged men alcoholics.

16

Medical/Surgical Disorders

A. The Hepatic Encephalopathies (a group of related brain dysfunctions: brain problems resulting from diseased liver function, including tiredness, coma, sharp rises in temperature, nosebleeds, and rectal bleeding)

B. Head trauma:
   1. Falls
   2. Fights
   3. Physical assaults
   4. Motor vehicle accidents
   5. Boating accidents

[See other chapters for other medical and surgical disorders.]

17

Sleep Disorders

A. Insomnia

B. Nightmares

C. Hallucinations while sleeping

D. Hypersomnolence (uncontrolled drowsiness; excessive sleeping)

E. Episodic nocturnal events (sleepwalking)

F. DIMS: Disorders of Initiating and Maintaining Sleep:
   1. Associated with and aggravates sleep apnea (loss of breathing while sleeping)
   2. Associated with and aggravates Alveolar Hypoventilation DIMS Syndrome (loss of breath; associated heart attacks)
   3. Associated with Restless Legs DIMS Syndrome and cramps of calf muscles ("Charlie horse")
   4. Associated with Myoclonus (twitching muscles)

G. Disorders of excessive somnolence (too much sleeping):
1. Narcolepsy (inability to stay awake)
2. Idiopathic CNS (central nervous system) Hypersomnolence (excessive sleep caused by alcoholism when no other causative factors can be found)
3. Associated with Kleine-Levin Syndrome (excessive hunger and drowsiness and twitching)

H. Disorders associated with parasomnias:
1. Sleepwalking
2. Sleep terrors
3. Sleep-related enuresis (bed wetting)
4. Dream anxiety attacks
5. Sleep-related epileptic seizures
6. Sleep-related bruxism (teeth grinding)
7. Sleep-related head banging
8. Impaired sleep-related penile tumescence (upon falling asleep, men normally get an erection)
9. Sleep-related painful erections
10. Sleep-related cluster headaches (migraine) and Chronic Paroxysmal Hemicrania (spasms on one side of the head)
11. Sleep-related abnormal swallowing syndrome
12. Sleep-related asthma
13. Sleep-related cardiovascular symptoms

14. Sleep-related gastroesophageal reflux (the contents of the stomach go into the esophagus during sleep, causing burning pain)

18

Peripheral and Autonomic Disorders

Peripheral (distal nerve) **Disorders:**
A. Polyneuropathy (tingling, numbness, and/or pain in fingers and toes)

B. Prominent axonal degeneration of myelinated and unmyelinated fibers (inability to grasp, write, and walk; damage to hands and feet)

Autonomic Nervous System (swallowing, heartbeat, dilation of small blood vessels, etc.) **Disorders:**
A. Anhydrosis (lack of sweating properly)

B. Impotence

C. Orthostatic Hypotension (dizziness or faintness when rising to a standing position)

D. Hypothermia (temperature regulation in the body is "off")

E. Hoarseness

F. Weak voice

G. Dysphagia (difficulty swallowing)

H. Urinary retention (trouble urinating)

I. Incontinence (inability to control urination)

J. Vocal cord paralysis in patients with Dysphonia (inability to speak)

K. Deterioration of primary peristalsis (deterioration of the function that moves food along in the intestines)

L. An abnormally low valsalva ratio (slowing of the pulse and decreased return of blood to the heart)

M. Patulous anal sphincter (inability to control the bowels)

N. Some cell nuclei show various stages of degeneration, from pyknosis (degeneration of body cells) to complete disappearance

19
Myopathy

Myopathic (muscle abnormality) **Disorders:**
A. Histological changes in muscles (cellular changes in the muscles, causing degeneration)

B. Myofibrillar Necrosis (dying muscle fibers)

C. Inflammation and Interstitial Fibrosis (swollen muscle that then becomes scarred and will not function correctly)

D. Muscle cell phosphorus deficiency

E. Low magnesium content

F. Depressed intercellular potassium

G. Increased contents of intracellular sodium, chloride, and calcium

H. Flank Muscle Necrosis (softness and wasting of the back muscles)

I. Hyperkalemia (increased calcium in the blood-stream, which can lead to muscle twitching and paralysis)

J. Acute Renal (kidney) Failure

K. Paralysis

L. Atrophic muscle fibers

M. Inflammation

N. Interstitial Fibrosis (decreased use of muscles because of scarring)

O. Congestive Heart Failure (the heart does not pump efficiently and fluid collects in the lungs)

P. Acute Rhabdomyolysis (disintegration of muscles, with decreased exercise ability)

Q. Fatal Myoglobinuria (death caused by muscle fibers breaking down and fragments getting into the kidneys)

R. Alteration of muscle enzymes

S. Interference with muscle blood flow

T. Interference with sodium transport

U. Direct structural damage to cells

20
Musculoskeletal Disturbances

A. Injuries and fractures:
  1. Mostly head injuries and fractures
  2. Accident-proneness (e.g., occurrence of more than one fracture within a two-year interval)
  3. Infection (complication of fractures). Alcohol compromises the body's ability to fight infections.

B. Limb Compression Syndrome (lack of blood flow into parts of the body, causing destruction of a whole limb or part of a limb)

C. Osteopenia (fragile, brittle bones)

D. Nontraumatic idiopathic osteonecrosis of the femoral head (destruction of the head of the femur [the hip] without prior injury)

21
Liver and Pancreas Disorders

Pancreatic Disorders:

A. Pancreatitis (severe pain in the abdomen; vomiting; diarrhea; high temperature). Can result in death, or in diabetes.

B. Biliary-Pancreatic Reflux (pancreatic enzymes go into the bile ducts and cause liver damage)

C. Obstruction-hypersecretion of the pancreas (dysfunction of pancreas, usually goes with pancreatitis)

D. Jaundice (yellowing of the skin)

E. Pancreatic exocrine insufficiency (insufficient enzymes available for breakdown of food)

F. Pancreatic ascites (fluid in abdomen)

G. Cirrhosis, with Portal Hypertension (liver disease, sometimes with bleeding from the esophagus, with bloated abdomen and yellowed skin)

Liver Disorders:

A. Hepatic insufficiency (liver does not perform its usual function of clearing body waste products; e.g., ammonia levels go up, leading to brain dysfunctions)

B. Hyperestrogenism (in males, an oversecretion of female hormones, leading to breast enlargement and testicular atrophy)

C. Coma

D. Jaundice

E. Spider Nevi (red blotches on the skin, resembling small spiders)

F. Pectoral Alopecia (loss of chest hair)

G. Liver damage

H. Ascites (swelling of the abdomen, secondary to fluid in the abdominal cavity, which is secondary to liver damage)

I. Altered hair distribution (body hair disappears)

J. Palmar Erythema (red palms without having had prior trauma)

K. Testicular atrophy (testes become small and soft)

L. Anemia (decrease in red blood cell count)

M. Hemorrhagic tendency (frequent bruising from minor trauma, bleeding under the skin, often because of liver damage)

N. Ankle Edema (swelling of the ankles, secondary to heart trouble and/or liver difficulties, both of which are frequently attributable to alcoholism)

O. Leukopenia (a decrease in white blood cells)

P. Thrombocytopenia (decrease in the number of blood platelets, leading to bleeding tendencies)

Q. Caput Medusae (dilated veins around the umbilicus, so-called because the veins resemble the head of the snake-haired Medusa; seen in infants and alcoholics)

R. Splenomegaly (enlarged spleen)

S. Hypersplenism (destructive functions of the spleen, leading to a deficiency of circulating blood elements, usually with splenic enlargement)

T. Esophageal Varices (bleeding from the tube that connects the throat and the stomach; usually inoperable and fatal)

U. Portal Hypertension Per Se (an abnormality of the arteries and veins leading to the liver, secondary to structural damage to the liver or the liver's inability to detoxify the blood)

22

Gastrointestinal Disorders

A. Reflux Esophagitis (contents of the stomach go into the esophagus, causing burning in the chest)

B. Carcinoma (cancer) of the esophagus

C. Gastritis (inflamed stomach)

D. Upper gastrointestinal bleeding

E. Acute Hemorrhagic Gastritis (acute bleeding of the stomach)

F. Mallory-Weiss Syndrome (vomiting blood from a tearing of the esophagus, secondary to severe vomiting, secondary in turn (often) to alcohol use)

G. Delayed gastric emptying (bloated stomach)

H. Chronic Atrophic Gastritis (chronically inflamed stomach)

I. Altered motility of the small intestine (food is not digested well)

J. Decreases in glycolytic enzymes (insufficient enzymes to break down food, resulting in malnutrition)

K. Increased triglyceride and cholesterol synthesis by intestinal slices (stomach problems increase the number of plaques in the heart, causing heart disease)

L. Decreased lactase activity

M. Decreased sucrase activity

N. Decreasing ATP (used in breaking down food) concentration

O. Cancer of the colon

23

Malnutrition and Related Nutritional Deficiencies

A. Avitaminosis (general, dangerous, chronic depletion of essential vitamins, including vitamin K, which is the clotting vitamin). Because of the lack of this vitamin, 25 percent of all alcoholics injured in auto accidents die, even though the accidents are often minor. They die from bleeding on the way to the hospital, because their blood does not possess the clotting ability.

B. Wernicke-Korsakoff Syndrome (defined on page 153)

C. Folate deficiency (contributes to chronic liver disease)

D. Vitamin B^6 deficiency (pyridoxine deficiency)

E. Magnesium deficiency

F. Zinc deficiency

G. Bone Disease

H. Cardiomyopathy (heart muscle becomes flabby and does not function well as a pump)

I. Beri-Beri (lack of thiamine [vitamin B^1], causing paralysis, edema, muscular wasting, mental deterioration, and finally heart failure; in wet beri-beri the person is too ill to do anything)

J. Anemia

K. Protein deficiency

L. Hypokalemia (not enough potassium, resulting in muscle twitching); can lead to heart problems.

M. Hypomagnesemia (low blood magnesium)

N. Cardiac Fibrosis (scarring of the heart muscle). Can lead to heart attacks.

O. Arrthythmias (irregular heartbeats)

P. Cardiomegaly (enlarged heart)

Q. Heart failure

R. Steatorrhea (fatty stools)

S. Osteomalacia (softening of bone, causing pain, tenderness, weakness, and nausea)

T. Metabolic Bone Disease (caused by a missing substance the bone needs to grow and stay healthy)

U. Scaling Dermatitis

V. Poor wound healing

W. Impaired taste

X. Night blindness (due in part to zinc deficiency from heavy drinking)

Y. Gout

24
Infectious Diseases

A. More frequent aspiration of pharyngeal contents into the lower airway during alcohol intoxication than occurs in sleep (people who are drunk vomit, and are unable to handle the secretions normally, thereby inhaling them, resulting in the secretions entering the lungs)

B. Depressed consciousness (difficulty in waking up)

C. Abnormal activity of the cilial escalator (inability to move foreign material from the lungs, the throat, and the mouth)

D. Reduced pulmonary clearance of organisms (inability of lungs to do away with invasive germs)

E. Reduced number of functioning neutrophils (reduced ability of bloodstream to fight infection)

F. Depleted serum phosphate (decrease in the normal blood constituents responsible for bone function)

G. Markedly impaired neutrophil chemotaxis (inability of the blood components to react to irritability responses, such as infection)

H. Increased serum concentrations of immunoglobulins (abnormal protein concentrations, leading to abnormal blood function)

I. Increased agglutination of *eshcerichia coli* and bacteriodes (inability of the bloodstream and its components to fight common blood infections)

J. Reduced hepatic clearance of antigen by a defective hepatic reticuloendothelial system (a malfunction of the blood contents, secondary to liver disease; i.e., the liver is unable to perform its normal functions cleansing the blood)

K. Depressed cell-mediated immunity (lack of body response to infections)

L. Protein malnutrition (a form of starvation)

M. Risks of infection for cirrhotic patients hospitalized because of gastrointestinal bleeding, Hepatic Encephalopathy (brain swelling), or

174

increasing ascites. Each of the following also carries a risk of infections that originate in the hospital (nosocomial infections):

1. Altered consciousness (loss of consciousness)
2. Vascular access devices (infections from i.v. fluids)
3. Indwelling bladder catheters
4. Surgery

N. Bacterial pneumonia

O. Bacterial meningitis

P. Endocarditis (infections of the lining of the inside of the heart)

Q. Altered closure of the epiglottis with aspiration of normal oropharyngeal bacteria into the lower airway (the usual safeguards against allowing the bacteria in the mouth to get into the lung area are missing or altered)

R. Lung abscess (secondary to stomach contents [vomit] getting into the lungs)

S. Empyema (infected fluid in the space between the lung and the ribs)

T. Bacteremia (a blood-carried bacterial infection)

U. Septic Arthritis (infection of the joints, secondary to bacteremia)

V. Purulent Pericarditis (infection of the covering of the heart, characterized by pus in the pericardial sac)

W. Cellulitis (skin infection)

X. Acute Purulent Bronchitis (infection of bronchial tubes, characterized by pus in the bronchi, usually with coughed-up yellow sputum; commonly related to cigarette smoking)

Y. Legionnaires' Disease, caused by *legionella pneumophilia*. Alcoholism is a risk factor for acquiring it.

Z. Pulmonary Tuberculosis (lung TB; more common in alcoholics)

A'. Spontaneous Bacterial Peritonitis (infection of the abdominal cavity, blood-borne, and without rupture of abdominal contents)

B'. Tuberculous Peritonitis (infection of abdominal cavity caused by tuberculosis)

25

Skin Diseases

A. Facial Edema (facial puffiness, seen usually in actively drinking alcoholics)

B. Tobacco smoke stains (person may hold onto a cigarette long enough to get burned). Alcohol affects skin so that it is more easily stained.

C. Rosacea (red blotches on face; skin redness)

D. Other pigmentation (liver spots; jaundice)

E. Spider Nevi (red blotches on the skin, resembling small spiders)

F. Skin flushing reactions

G. Generalized Pruritis (itching)

H. Glossitis (tongue inflammation)

I. Feminine hair pattern in men

J. Miscellaneous skin problems

K. Dermatitis (inflammation of the skin, often with itching)

L. Keratosis (skin growths)

M. Drug eruption (skin changes, secondary to medication or drug use [like antibiotics, often]; alcoholics may become allergic to them and/or get skin itching, burning, and hives)

N. Psoriasis (a skin disease)

O. Onychomycosis (a fungus disease of the fingernails and toenails: the nails become thick, white, opaque and brittle)

P. Alcoholic Ulcero-Osteolytic Neuropathy (bone ulcers due to lack of nerve supply to the bones, from alcoholism)

Q. Pellagra (nutritional skin disease)

R. Zinc deficiency (contributes to pellagra)

S. Porphyria (urinary tract infection, due to an abnormal element in the blood and urine; often associated with liver disease)

T. Mutilating Skin Disease (terrible scarring of the skin, abdominal pain, and brain changes)

26

Effects of Alcohol
on the Hematopoietic System

Hematopoietic System (blood cell-forming)
Disorders:

A. Anemia (low hemoglobin)

B. Leukopenia (low white blood cell count; may show up as infection)

C. Thrombocytopenia (low platelet count; may show up as skin rash)

D. Megaloblastosis (shows up as poor healing)

E. Pathological Sideroblasts (shows up as infections, difficulty in healing, and nervous disorders)

F. Folate deficiency (shows up with decreased healing and general poor health)

180

G. Sideroblastic Anemia (shows up as paleness and feeling bad)

H. Hemolytic Anemia (same as above)

I. Iron Deficiency Anemia (same as above)

J. Drop in serum folate (same as above)

K. Decreased levels of vitamin K-dependent coagulation factors (decreased ability to clot blood and control bleeding)

27

Reproductive System Disorders

A. Testicular atrophy (testes become small and soft)

B. Decreased libido (lessened sexual drive)

C. Impotence

D. Infertility

E. Hyperestrogenism (female changes in men)

F. Female Escutcheon (men begin to have female pubic hair patterns)

G. Gynecomastia (enlargement of male breasts)

H. Palmar Erythema (red palms)

I. Spider Angiomata (red, spider-like splotches on the skin)

J. Spermatozoal morphological abnormalities (lead to infertility)

K. Inadequate secretion of follicle-stimulating hormone and luteinizing hormone (in women, skin, hair, and menstrual changes)

L. Menstrual disorders

M. Vaginal infections

N. Infertility

O. Repeated miscarriages

28

Effects on the Fetus

Fetal Alcohol Syndrome:
A. Retarded growth

B. Neurological abnormality

C. Developmental delay

D. Intellectual impairment

E. Microcephaly (small head at birth)

F. Microphthalmia (abnormally small eyeball)

G. Short palpebral fissures (eyelids come together)

H. Poorly developed philtrum (deformed nose)

I. Adverse effects on almost every organ system in the fetus

29

Endocrine Disturbances

A. Reduced Growth Hormone Response: Contributes to anything from diabetes to bone disease.

B. Gynecomastia (see page 182)

C. Hypoandrogenism (demasculinization)

D. Hyperestrogenism (feminization)

E. Alcohol-induced water diuresis (tremendous amount of urinary output)

30

Respiratory System Disorders

A. Lung infections

B. Diminished Gag Reflex (inability to control swallowing)

C. Depressed cough (inability to cough completely)

D. Chronic Bronchitis

E. Chronic Obstructive Airway Disease (failure to breathe efficiently enough because breathing tubes are narrowed from chronic irritation due to tobacco smoking, which often accompanies alcoholic drinking)

F. Pneumonia

G. Suppurative lung diseases (with pus)

H. Pulmonary Tuberculosis (lung TB; there is a higher incidence of this among alcoholics)

I. Maldistribution between ventilation and blood flow

J. Damage of lung parenchyma (lung structure)

K. Aspiration Pneumonia (from breathing in one's vomit)

L. Bronchiectasis (infection of the bronchial tubes)

M. Lung abscess

N. Wheezing

O. Dyspnea (shortness of breath)

P. Shock

Q. Edema

R. Bacterial infection

S. Laryngeal and Esophageal Carcinoma (cancer)

T. Sustained Pulmonary Hypertension (heart disease caused by an abnormal exchange of blood between the heart and the lung; usually fatal)

31

Cardiovascular System Disorders

Please Note: The first five disorders are degenerative changes in the heart's components—muscle, nerve supply, blood supply, coverings—that adversely affect the functioning of the heart, and usually lead to death:

A. Damaged myocardial cells (subtle or overt)

B. Hydropic and fatty and hyaline degeneration

C. Areas of degeneration

D. Fibrosis

E. Endocardial thickening

Other Cardiovascular Problems:

F. Reduction in contractility

G. Enhanced cardiovascular reflex modulation (significant in particularly unhealthy alcoholics who may have underlying cardiac disease)

H. Increased oxygen requirements

I. Tachycardia (fast heartbeat)

J. Elevated systolic and diastolic blood pressure (changed blood pressure due to reduced heart function)

K. Primary Myocardial Disease (disease of the heart muscle)

L. Cardiac Arrythmias (irregular heartbeat)

M. Angina Pectoris (chest pain, secondary to coronary orischemic heart disease)

N. Myocardial Infarction (heart attack)

O. Cerebral Vascular Accident (strokes)

P. Hypertension (high blood pressure)

32
Trauma and Surgery Problems

A. Laceration (cuts that bleed; often profusely in an alcoholic)

B. Skull fractures (increased tendencies toward this in alcoholics)

C. Subdural Hematoma (brain blood clots)

D. Cancer of oropharynx or larynx

E. Rhinophyma (enlarged, deformed noses)

F. Gallstones

G. Esophageal Cancer

H. Spontaneous rupture of esophagus (occurs from alcoholics' continual vomiting)

I. Fractured ribs

J. Hemorrhoids

K. Hepatoma (primary cancer of the liver)

L. Dupuytren's Contracture (hand deformities)

M. Venous leg ulcers (caused by varicose veins, which occur in most alcoholics)

N. Bilateral frostbite (occurs when alcoholics stay outside improperly clothed in cold weather)

33

Psychiatric Disorders and Alcoholism

A. Depression

B. Denial

C. Anger

D. Guilt

E. Shame

F. Alcohol withdrawal

G. Feelings of omnipotence

H. Self-care incapacity

I. Anhedonia (inability to experience happiness)

J. Bipolar Disorder (manic depression)

K. Unipolar Affective Disorder (mania or depression)

L. Borderline Personality Disorder

M. Pathological narcissism

N. Jealousy

O. Schizophrenia

P. Sociopathy

Q. Suicide

R. Marital dysfunction

*   *   *   *   *

In addition to the above listings in these chapters, alcoholics who survive these diseases tend to experience early onset of many or all of the many dozens of aging processes.

Guide for Help

If you would like information about meeting schedules, literature and other services of Alcoholics Anonymous, Al-Anon or Al-Ateen in your area, simply call Directory Assistance in your area code and ask for the number. They will be happy to have someone return your call and help you in any way they can.

The author, Toby Rice Drews, is a counselor and social worker and she is available for counseling family members. You may reach her at her home in Baltimore, MD, at (301) 243-8352.

Audiocassettes, films, newsletters, and other resources by Toby Rice Drews are available from:

Maryland Publishing
P.O. Box 19910
Baltimore, MD 21211

All of Toby's books are available
in caselots at special prices.

Any organization involved with helping
alcoholics and their families
interested in bulk order discounts can contact:

BRIDGE PUBLISHING, INC.
1-800-631-5802

Or write:
BRIDGE PUBLISHING, INC.
2500 Hamilton Blvd.
South Plainfield, NJ 07080

Educators, counselors, and health professionals
may obtain a catalog of educational aids by sending
$2.00 to:

THE HEALTH CONNECTION
Narcotics Education Incorporated
6830 Laurel Street, N.W.
Washington, D.C. 20012
USA